Real-Life Case Studies for Teachers

William Hayes

Rowman & Littlefield Education

Lanham • New York • Toronto • Plymouth, UK

Published in the United States of America
by Rowman & Littlefield Education
A Division of Rowman & Littlefield Publishers, Inc.
A wholly owned subsidiary of The Rowman & Littlefield Publishing Group, Inc.
4501 Forbes Boulevard, Suite 200, Lanham, Maryland 20706
www.rowmaneducation.com

Estover Road
Plymouth PL6 7PY
United Kingdom

British Cataloguing in Publication Information Available

Library of Congress Cataloguing-in-Publication Data

Hayes, William, 1938–
   Real-life case studies for teachers / William Hayes.
p. cm.
   ISBN 13: 978-0-8108-3748-5
   ISBN 10: 0-8108-3748-X
   1. Teachers—United States—Case Studies. 2. Teaching—
United States—Case Studies. I. Title.
LB1775.2.H39   2000
71.102—dc21

Contents

Preface

Preparing students to be teachers has never been easy. As a result of significant research in recent years, teacher education programs have important new information and skills to offer prospective members of the profession. Instruction in brain research, multiple intelligence, learning styles, and authentic assessment can enhance a teacher's effectiveness in the classroom. Still, it continues to be said that education courses in college do not fully prepare teachers for the dilemmas they will face in our diverse, bureaucratic and often conflict-ridden schools.

This book is first of all an attempt to introduce students in education classes to a variety of problems that they might face as teachers. Using the situations described in these case studies, college instructors can guide students as they seek answers to these dilemmas. The cases are varied and deal with real-life situations that teachers have faced and will face in the classrooms of our country.

There is little question that the discussions that will ensue from reading these cases will enliven education classes that have often been considered by students to be pedantic and dull. More importantly, they will cause students to engage in creative problem-solving. Such an exercise provides excellent practice for the kinds of questions that are being asked in teacher certification examinations. These tests frequently present questions that require students to react to situations encountered in a school. Under the tutelage of an experienced professor, students can be shown the best ways to approach the problems outlined in this book.

Perhaps the best way to use these case studies is as a supplement to the main text in a survey course such as Foundations of Education. The table of contents, beginning on page iii, identifies the primary themes of each case study. When the instructor is teaching about a certain topic, the contents will identify appropriate case studies to use. Each case study begins with an introductory paragraph that explains in more detail the subject of the selection.

The case studies can be assigned to individuals or groups of students who are charged with sharing with the entire class both the facts of the case and a preferred solution. It is also possible to assign the cases to the entire class prior to a class discussion. The Possible Discussion Questions at the end of each case can provide the basis for class dialogue.

Having used case studies to enliven classes for years, I can guarantee that students will be interested and responsive. This method of teaching is a way to bring real-life problems into the college classroom. Since there are no easy answers to the questions raised by the cases, they will help students to better understand the ambiguities and difficulties they will face as teachers.

Acknowledgments

I would like to acknowledge the valuable assistance of several individuals in helping to prepare this publication. Kristen Bianchi, a student secretary in the Teacher Education Division at Roberts Wesleyan College, not only typed the manuscript, but also acted as an in-house editor for the project. Her work was invaluable and made this book possible. Finally, I would again thank my wife Nancy, whose patience, proofreading, and insightful suggestions were essential to the completion of this project.

Case Study 1

She Really Is a Good Kid

According to numerous research studies, cheating is widespread in our schools. Although all schools frown upon the practice and attempt to establish rules that will punish students, enforcing these rules is almost always the responsibility of the classroom teacher. Since academic dishonesty can take many forms, it is difficult to develop policies that will cover every situation. Statements found in faculty handbooks are often general in nature and offer few guidelines as to what a teacher should do when cheating is suspected.

Linda Schultz was in her first year as a fifth-grade teacher in the Pembroke Elementary School. Like all first-year teachers, she had experienced both good days and bad days during her first eight months in the district, and now that she had survived until April she was feeling much better about her class. During September and October, she had felt very anxious and even had trouble sleeping at night. Having her own class had proven much more challenging than student teaching. As a student teacher, she had not experienced parents second-guessing her, nor did she really struggle with classroom management. Linda now realized that the primary reason she had so little trouble with discipline then was that her master teacher had set the tone for the class before Linda had ever taught a lesson. The students had loved and respected the master teacher, Mrs. Henderson, and Linda had benefited from the environment that had been established in the classroom.

When she was faced with twenty-five of her own fifth graders on the first day of school, it was a new challenge for Linda. As she looked back on these first few weeks, she now knew that she had worried too much about whether the children would like her. When she finally decided to become more assertive, there had been several students, and even parents, who objected to her stricter discipline.

One of the worst incidents was when she telephoned Angela Canon's mother. Angela had repeatedly challenged Linda every time she was disciplined. The student was often disrespectful and defiant, and Linda had thought that perhaps a

1

call to her home would lead to some parental support. What she received instead was an angry tongue-lashing from Mrs. Canon on Linda's inability to control her classroom and subsequent picking on certain students. The most frequent victim was Angela and Mrs. Canon said she was "tired of hearing about unfair treatment." On several occasions, Angela had told her mother that Miss Schultz "never yells at Cindy Tomidy" and that "when I'm talking to Cindy, Miss Schultz always picks on me, just because Cindy's father is a doctor and my father is only a truck driver."

After her conversation with Angela's mother, Linda learned that all was not well in the Canon household. Angela's father was a truck driver, and that past summer he had left on a job but had not returned. Instead, he had sent Mrs. Canon a letter saying that he needed time to think about their marriage and that he would contact her when he had made a decision. Ten months had passed without a word and both the mother and her daughter were very worried about their future. There was barely enough income from Mrs. Canon's secretarial job to support the two of them.

Cindy Tomidy, on the other hand, had everything she needed and more. Like her friend Angela, Cindy was attractive, but unlike Angela, she had the most stylish clothing. Her family was very close and they lived in one of the nicest houses in town. Cindy was also a straight-A student. It had surprised Linda when she looked at Angela's past records that she too had been an excellent student in the early grades. As a fifth grader, she had become inconsistent about doing her work and seemed not to care about studying for tests. As a result, her grades were no better than a C in most subjects.

Despite their different backgrounds, the girls had been friends since kindergarten and remained close as they were about to enter their teenage years. The two ate lunch together every day and Angela was frequently invited to the Tomidy home. Especially this year, the Tomidys had made a point of including Angela in their family outings.

As the year progressed, Angela had behaved more positively and had become more cooperative, so Linda was both surprised and upset when she read the multicultural research paper that Angela handed in. As part of their study of different countries, the students were assigned to write a paper about the European country of their choice. Although more than one student could choose a country, they were told that they were to work alone and discover their own sources. The final paper must be their own work. The papers prepared by Cindy and Angela dealt with Poland and a simple check of their bibliographies showed that they were almost identical; the texts of the papers were also similar, with whole paragraphs being identical. Having read their work for almost a year, Linda was quite certain that the sentence and word choice identified the work as Cindy's writing. Despite their teacher's admonitions, the students had turned in work that was too much alike.

After reading both papers several times, Linda knew that she had to do something. Should she first talk to the children? At what point, if any, should the parents be involved? Reading through the faculty handbook, it was clear that it was the policy of the district to teach and enforce academic honesty. Other than expressing the seriousness of the issue, the policy gave no specific guidelines to teachers on how to deal with cheating. Linda also considered seeking the advice of her principal, Mr. Luskey. She was hesitant to do so at this stage, but knew that she had to act.

POSSIBLE DISCUSSION QUESTIONS

1. Should schools attempt to develop a standard policy to cover incidents involving academic dishonesty? If so, what form might such a policy take?

2. What do you feel Linda should do in this case?

Case Study 2

The Observation

All teachers have experienced formal observations by their school administrators. Sometimes the principal or department chairperson comes into the classroom unannounced, and on other occasions, advance notice is given. For some teachers, any classroom observation can be a stressful experience. In most schools, a faculty member is observed no more than three times a year, so each visit is of some importance. This is especially true if the instructor is being considered for tenure. Whether the experience is traumatic or not can also be affected by the administrator who is doing the evaluation. Faculty members often learn in advance the type of lesson that is most likely to impress their principal, and with pre-arranged observations, teachers often feel that they are expected to do a special lesson.

There is another source of conflict caused by formal observations. Theoretically, one of the reasons for the observation is to help teachers improve their instructional techniques, but unfortunately, most teachers and many administrators see the real purpose of the process to be the evaluation of the teacher. This being the case, many teachers face the dilemma of whether to teach a typical lesson or to "put on a show."

Bob Mulaney is an eighth-grade American history teacher at the Lincoln Middle School. Well into his second year of a three-year probationary period, Bob enjoyed his work and was feeling much better about his teaching. During his first year in the school, he had tried too hard to be a friend to his students. This desire, along with his lack of experience, caused him to have some classroom management problems. Miss Stevens, his principal, had been helpful and this year he felt much more in control of his classroom. Even though she had been sympathetic, he knew she was somewhat concerned about him as a probationary teacher. The issue of whether or not he would be offered tenure was still in question.

Bob's first observation this year had taken place the second week in October. The students had behaved fine, but it had been a lackluster lesson. The principal had included in her report a number of suggestions on how he could have done a better job engaging the students. Still, with his classes under control, Bob was

4

confident he was improving as a teacher every week and that he was capable of someday becoming a master teacher. There certainly had been a number of days this year when he had excited the class with special activities and lessons.

On the other hand, his principal had been a creative and innovative social studies teacher and well versed in the subject. He was somewhat intimidated whenever she entered his classroom and when he received the note after lunch last Friday that she would be formally observing him on the following Thursday, he had trouble concentrating during his final two classes of the afternoon.

It was now Sunday evening and Bob was sitting at his desk in his apartment. The Sunday afternoon football games were over and it was time to plan for next weeks' classes. According to the two-week unit plan that he had drawn up the previous Sunday, the class was to complete the study of the United States Constitution on Monday, Tuesday, and Wednesday of next week. His schedule called for a day of review for all classes on Thursday and the next unit test was to be given on Friday. As there was pressure to complete the entire course of study, American history teachers were forced to maintain a careful schedule. The students were expected to take a comprehensive test on all of American history at the end of the year, so Bob had developed a schedule that would allow him to complete the course of study and still leave ten days for review. Although he had worked hard to meet the schedule, he was already several days behind.

Studying the Constitution with his eighth graders had not proven nearly as exciting as the activities he had developed when they studied the American Revolution. During that unit, he had done some role-playing activities which had been very popular with the students. As he thought about the week ahead, he was concerned that the students would be tired of talking about delegated and reserved powers and that the review session he had planned on Thursday could be very boring.

He had thought about an activity to end the unit which would feature a mock Constitutional ratification debate. Some students would take the part of the Federalists and others would be the Anti-Federalists. Bob was hopeful that such a debate would create a spirited discussion involving all of the students. However, because preparation for the debate would take two or three days, he had discarded the idea.

Now he was thinking that such a debate would be just the kind of lesson that would impress Miss Stevens. However, he had not done much cooperative learning with his students and they had not done any real research. He wondered if they could successfully carry out such a debate and questioned whether six or eight of the students could be induced to participate in a debate in front of their peers. The debate idea was definitely a risk. It could turn out to be an outstanding learning activity or it could fail, and then there was still his schedule to worry about.

If he could somehow start the students preparing for the debate on Monday, they might be ready to make a presentation by Thursday, but he was not quite sure what to do with the remainder of the class during those days. Perhaps they could be part of a research team for either the Federalists or the anti-Federalists. On

Thursday, they could also be partisans who would ask questions of the opposing debate team. He could set up the debate as a local town meeting in Lincoln during the year 1787.

If he chose to alter his schedule, it would then be necessary to finish teaching the unit on Friday and Monday. That would allow him to review the following Tuesday and give his unit test on Wednesday. This plan would put him three days off his schedule, but he thought that he could catch up later in the course. Bob was feeling strongly that he needed to "hit a home run" with this observation to show Miss Stevens that he could not only manage a classroom, but also teach creatively. He had almost convinced himself to alter his schedule when his conservative nature began to make him question the new plan.

Bob wondered if he was merely staging a show to help ensure that he would receive tenure or if the debate was really designed to help students learn about the Constitution. Couldn't a well-structured review lesson be just as impressive? Why was he worrying about being impressive, anyway? In any case, if he was going to change his plans for the week, he would have to make the decision now.

POSSIBLE DISCUSSION QUESTIONS

1. What do you think the primary purpose of teacher observation should be? What do you think the chief objective is in most school districts?

2. What do you think Bob should do in the class in which he will be observed?

Reorganizing a Classroom

With the passage of Public Law 94-142 in 1975, many public schools chose to place those students needing special education in self-contained classrooms. Often, the classrooms were located a distance away from the child's community school. Recently, pressure from parents, government officials, and the courts has resulted in these students being assigned to regular classrooms in their neighborhood schools. This practice, known as inclusion, has created new challenges for the classroom teacher. In many cases, these teachers are being asked to educate young people who are severely physically handicapped or mentally retarded. Special education teachers and counselors, along with speech, physical, and occupational therapists, are assigned to help the students, and a classroom teacher may also be given a teacher aide. The difficulty is how to organize a classroom to effectively use this extra help.

Sally Landers had been teaching fourth grade for sixteen years. Although she had done some team teaching with the other fourth-grade teachers, nothing in her experience had prepared her for the inclusion program her school district had recently adopted. Primarily because of pressure from a group of parents of students who were receiving special education, the district had decided to assign twenty-three of its thirty-two most handicapped students back into their neighborhood schools. The principals of these schools had chosen the teachers who they thought could best work with these children, and Sally had been selected to have three inclusion children in her class that fall.

The previous spring, the teachers in the district who would be receiving special education students were sent to a three-day workshop on inclusion. During the meeting, Sally had learned about the history of special education, the laws currently governing special education, and about the rationale supporting inclusion. She also was exposed to some limited research that had been done on the practice of including severely handicapped children in a regular classroom. This had all been very interesting, but the sessions had included very little practical help on how to organize an inclusion classroom.

In analyzing her class for the coming year, Sally was pleased that she would only have nineteen students. It would be much easier to deal with this number, rather than the typical twenty-five or twenty-six children which characterized most regular classrooms. On the other hand, the three special education students she would receive would create a very special challenge. Included would be John, a paraplegic wheelchair student who could not write or even move his arms. Lenora was a mentally retarded student with an IQ of less than sixty who had a severe speech problem, and needed to work with both the physical and occupational therapists. The third student, Billy, had severe learning disabilities and had not yet reached the first-grade reading level or learned to write anything but his first name. Most challenging was the fact that he had been a severe behavior problem for his previous teachers. His Individualized Education Plan (IEP) called for frequent counseling sessions.

In thinking about how she should organize her classroom for the coming year, Sally had listed the individuals who would be working with her class:

1. A half-time teacher aide.
2. A half-time special education teacher.
3. A speech therapist who would be serving two of her students.
4. A remedial reading teacher who would be serving one student.
5. An occupational therapist who would be serving two students.
6. A physical therapist who would be serving one student.
7. A counselor who would be serving all three special education students.

Sally knew that the IEPs of her three students specifically mandated the services of these specialists and that if all of the services were provided on a "pull out" basis, her new students would be out of the classroom for a considerable amount of the school day.

In her reading, she had learned that sometimes the work of the specialist could be done in the regular classroom and that other students could benefit. Although this was a possibility, Sally was not sure how it would work in practice. She also was somewhat concerned about how she would utilize the teacher aide. Having never worked with an aide, she was not sure whether the new assistant would work only with the special education students or with the entire class. Of course, her primary concern was how she was going to integrate her three special students into the regular classroom activities. Specifically, she was worried about Billy and the possible disruption he might bring to the classroom.

Knowing that the first day of school was only two weeks away, Sally had decided to call a meeting with everyone who would be working in her classroom. The purpose of the session would be to talk about a schedule and try to determine the best way to meet the needs of all the students. She was both delighted and surprised when everyone she invited agreed to attend the meeting that was scheduled for 3:00 the next day. She would meet privately with her aide, Judy Adams, an hour earlier.

In preparing for the group meeting, Sally was not exactly sure of what role she should play. Should she consider herself the chief executive officer of the classroom and present a schedule? Or could she act as a nondirective coordinator and try to bring about a compromise schedule that would be acceptable to all the members of the team? Should she strongly encourage the specialist to work within the classroom in order to benefit all the students? The alternative was to schedule times for her three special students to be taken out of the classroom. Was it up to her to make the final decision on the schedule? What would be the role of the half-time special education teacher? Would she work only with the three students or would she team teach with Sally? Should the classroom team participate in the optional volunteer aide program which brought parents and senior citizens into classrooms? Would this merely add to the confusion? These questions plagued Sally as she prepared for the meeting. She wished that she had been given the opportunity the previous year to visit inclusion classrooms in neighboring school districts, but the timing of the decision had made that impossible. As a result of her lack of experience with inclusion, Sally had more questions than answers. Usually a confident person, she was feeling very uneasy about the meeting she had called.

POSSIBLE DISCUSSION QUESTIONS

1. How should Sally deal with her new aide? What are the special duties that aides should be expected to perform in an elementary classroom?

2. What is the proper role for a classroom teacher when dealing with other professionals who are serving students in his or her classroom?

3. Prepare an agenda for the meeting that Sally will be conducting.

Case Study 4

Teachers vs. Administration

Teachers have long sought recognition as professionals. At the same time, in order to assure fair compensation and conditions of employment, they have become associated with organized labor. In doing so, teachers have sometimes adopted labor union tactics to help them achieve their demands. While they desire to be considered in the same category as doctors, lawyers, and accountants, their behavior and associations have sometimes led them to be compared with construction workers and teamsters. This dichotomy often places individual teachers in difficult situations. On one hand, they wish to be loyal to their students and school, but they also want to cooperate with their peers who are attempting to improve salaries and working conditions. As a result, teachers are sometimes in a position where difficult choices have to be made.

Amy had been shaken by the conversation that had just taken place in the faculty room. As a twelve-year veteran of several contract negotiations, she had never experienced a more stressful period within the district. The contract between the Board of Education and the teachers had expired nine months ago and little progress had been made toward resolving the impasse. The primary issue was financial, and the district was maintaining its position that it could only afford a two-percent raise for each of the next three years. The negotiator for the district pointed out that, because state aid was not likely to increase in the near future, the only way extra money could be made available would be to increase the property tax. Given the current economic situation, the board argued that any attempt to raise property taxes more than the rate of inflation would be vehemently opposed by a majority of the district's citizens.

The faculty negotiating team continually pointed out that the cost of living index had risen almost four percent during the past twelve months, and what the board was offering would not even keep up with that increase. Although Amy's husband Ron earned a very substantial salary as an engineer, she was very concerned about another district proposal. Secondary school teachers now had two free periods each day to provide the teachers time to prepare lessons, grade papers, and to meet and help students. Granted, some teachers spent much of this time drinking coffee in the faculty room, but for Amy, the periods were important as the work that she accomplished during the day did not have to be taken home in the evening. She was currently spending an hour or two each school night on work from school, and any more time spent on work at home would be time taken away from her husband and children.

The district saw the reduction of a free period for each teacher as a way of eliminating a number of paid teacher aides who were currently doing hall duty, cafeteria monitoring, and proctoring study halls. Along with saving money, the Board of Education and the superintendent were arguing that such eliminations would improve overall discipline in the school. Both parties agreed that some of the aides had proven to be less than effective as disciplinarians. The superintendent believed that the school had been a more secure and disciplined institution before the teachers had been given two free periods in a contract signed six years ago. He was convinced that aides would never do the supervision duties as well as teachers and he very much wanted to return to more professional supervision.

These two issues had created within the Faculty Association a unity and determination that had never existed in the past. Teachers had already picketed the fall concert and an evening football game, distributing pamphlets that explained the Faculty Association's position in the contract negotiations. These demonstrations were due in large part to the school district's use of its October newsletter to describe the current impasse in a way that the teachers thought was unfair. Now there was a public relations struggle with both sides seeking to affect public opinion.

Amy had explained to the leadership of the Association that she had been unable to participate in any of the picketing because she was visiting her ailing mother at the nursing home. She knew that she could not continue to use this excuse and that she would soon have to make a decision on how she was going to react to the current contract dilemma. In fact, there were three separate decisions she would have to make during the next two weeks.

Picketing was now planned for the next Board of Education meeting, and the Faculty Association was contacting each teacher individually to plead for participation. The group would carry signs in front of the building before the meeting and then march into the building as a unit just prior to the session. From the discussion in the faculty room, it seemed to Amy that most of her colleagues were planning to attend. She could not imagine herself carrying a picket sign or marching into the meeting as part of a militant union. Her father had been a manager at a local factory and Amy had grown up with an anti-union bias. She could not imagine herself carrying a picket sign or marching into a meeting as part of a militant union, and being part of such an activity was not something she wanted to do.

A second tactic of the association also bothered her. They had ordered several hundred maroon T-shirts that said "Teachers deserve a fair contract." The plan was that all of the teachers would wear these shirts to school every Friday until the contract was signed. As a person who prided herself in wearing fine clothing to work, the thought of teaching in a maroon T-shirt seemed to Amy very unprofessional. Also, she didn't really understand how wearing the shirts in class would help teachers to sign a better contract. Although some students were sympathetic with the teachers' position, others, perhaps affected by their parents' views, were antagonistic. Although Amy felt bringing dispute into the classroom could be disruptive and even counterproductive, she knew that most of her colleagues would wear the shirts to school.

Finally, her most immediate problem was the dance on Friday evening. School policy called for a minimum of one faculty member to join with parents and administrators in chaperoning a dance. Amy had been asked to be the faculty chaperon and had not yet given a final answer. She was well aware that almost every teacher in the school had been asked and no one had agreed to attend.

Although there had been no formal request from the Faculty Association that teachers not do these extra duties, there was a clear understanding among the teachers that not volunteering for extra duties would send a message to the district that the contract should be settled. Yesterday, the principal had put out a memo saying that if a faculty member did not agree to chaperone, the dance would be canceled. The vice president of the Student Council, which was sponsoring the dance, had asked to meet with Amy after school. The student had already shared that there were no other faculty members who were likely to volunteer, so if Amy did not agree, it appeared that there would be no dance. If she attended the dance, a number of Amy's peers would interpret the gesture as a lack of support for the Faculty Association's position.

POSSIBLE DISCUSSION QUESTIONS

1. Should Amy agree to chaperone the dance?

2. Should she wear the T-shirt to school on Fridays?

3. Should she be part of the demonstration at the Board of Education meeting?

4. What tactics used by teachers' unions during a contract dispute would you be likely to support?

5. What tactics used by teachers' unions during a contract dispute would you be unlikely to support?

Case Study 5

The Noisy Classroom

Dealing with one's colleagues is an important part of any job. Teaching is no longer an isolated activity that allows the instructor to close the door to the outside world, and educators are increasingly engaged in cooperative planning and team teaching. When a team member does not fit well into the group, it can have significant effects on everyone involved, including the students. Experienced teachers have a professional obligation to help new teachers in acquiring new skills. In this case study, these issues come together to create a dilemma for a veteran teacher.

It was December and the situation had not improved. Carol Ward had been teaching for almost thirty years and she had never faced a problem like this. Once again, the noise in the classroom next door was so loud that it was disturbing her third-grade math lesson. Carol also suspected that the commotion was affecting her students' ability to concentrate, and it had been like this almost since the beginning of the school year. Not only could she hear the students shouting, she frequently heard the teacher, Jennifer Lundy, almost screaming directions above the apparent anarchy. Carol was also aware that Miss Lundy's students were coming and going from the classroom on a regular basis.

Concerned about the almost constant high noise level, Carol had asked Jennifer on at least three occasions if she could help the young teacher. As an experienced educator, Carol was aware that a recent college graduate just beginning her professional career might have trouble during her first year of teaching, but Jennifer had not been willing to accept an offer of help.

Perhaps part of the problem was that Jennifer had not been hired until the last week in August, and had had little time to prepare for her first position. Normally, the administration would have included Carol and Natalie Allen, the other third-grade teacher, in the interview process. Both of the returning teachers were on vacation, however, so Bob Blaney, the principal, had chosen Jennifer from a limited list of candidates. Carol was quite certain that, had she been involved in the selection, she might have noticed Jennifer's shyness and lack of assertiveness.

13

Even though Carol might doubt the wisdom of hiring Jennifer, she and Natalie were trying to be helpful, but so far the young teacher was unfortunately keeping her problems to herself. In the weekly meetings of the three third-grade teachers, Jennifer said very little. In the past, it had been the practice of the team to occasionally schedule large group instruction. For these lessons, the portable walls of the classroom were opened and the three third grades were brought together for special activities. Carol was very interested in social studies and on a weekly basis used various media to teach the combined classes. As part of these lessons, students were divided into smaller groups for discussion. She had been doing these lessons for years and the students almost always reacted in a positive way. Natalie had done the same with special science classes for the combined groups. The previous teacher had taught health studies in this way, and in late September, Jennifer had agreed to carry on this role with a group lesson on the respiratory system. At the beginning of the class, she had been unable to get the attention of the large group, and the experienced teachers had to intervene to restore order. Since that experience, Jennifer had not volunteered to do another group lesson and both Carol and Natalie were concerned that the third graders were getting behind in health studies.

As the only administrator, Bob Blaney had a staff of over thirty professionals and his schedule was extremely busy. This semester, especially, he was spending long hours at the central office preparing for a bond issue which would allow the construction of an addition to the building. In any case, he had yet to schedule an observation of his new third-grade teacher and Carol was quite sure that the principal was unaware of Jennifer's classroom management problem.

Problems like this had led to a great deal of discussion during the previous year about establishing a formal mentoring program for new teachers. The idea had been to assign an experienced member of the faculty to all of the nontenured teachers who would help the new teachers adjust to their responsibilities, both in and out of the classroom. Unfortunately, the idea was not implemented during the negotiations for a new contract. The teachers' union had taken the position that the mentors should be compensated, but the Board of Education negotiator had argued that helping newcomers was part of a teacher's professional responsibility. Such a program, had it been instituted, might have mandated that an experienced teacher could observe and offer helpful advice to a new teacher.

Even without such a formal program, Carol wanted to be helpful to Jennifer. She thought that the young woman wanted help, but was either too proud or too shy to ask. Whatever the reason, it seemed that the administration would soon begin to receive calls from some concerned parents. It was also possible that an accident might occur in a classroom that was constantly in an uproar.

The easy thing to do would be merely to inform the principal and to make it his problem, but knowing her administrator, Carol expected that Bob would treat the situation as a crisis. She would really rather try to deal with the situation herself. Natalie, whose classroom was not adjacent to Jennifer's, was not nearly as concerned and believed that these were typical first-year teacher problems. Natalie had even suggested that to survive, Jennifer would have to win the battle on her own. In the long run, Natalie believed that "Some of us make it and some of us don't, and I am not gong to lose any sleep over Jennifer. If she wants help, all she has to do is ask." Carol really wanted to help Jennifer, but was unsure of how to go about it and wondered if it was even her job to try.

POSSIBLE DISCUSSION QUESTIONS

1. Does Carol have a responsibility to report the problem to the principal?

2. Is a formal mentor program for new teachers a positive idea? How might it work?

3. How would you suggest Carol might go about trying to help the young teacher?

To Retain or Not to Retain

Ever since students have been placed in grade-level classes, there has been a debate over whether it is an acceptable and appropriate educational practice to retain students at a grade level for a second year. Arguments about so-called "social promotions" have occurred in many schools. With increased pressure for students to obtain mastery and to meet even higher standards, the debates about students repeating grades are likely to continue. Although there is significant research on the issue of retention, parents and educators continue to grapple with the issue.

Beth Streeter was eight years old and in two months would complete her third-grade year. Socially, she was an outgoing young lady with a number of friends in her class. Although she was quite well adjusted socially, she had not done well academically. Her recent reading scores showed her performing at just above the second-grade level. While her classmates were writing complete sentences and even paragraphs, Beth's skills as a writer were more comparable to those of a first grader than a student completing third grade. Although she showed great aptitude in art, her grades in other subjects were a C minus or lower.

Her teachers had requested that Beth be tested by the school psychologist and he had concluded that the child did not "legally qualify for special education services." In his report, it was suggested that a volunteer might work with the girl during her free time. An attempt was made to carry out the recommendation, but Beth had resisted because she had wanted to use her free time to be with her classmates. The senior citizen volunteer had become discouraged after several sessions and had stopped coming to the classroom.

Beth also seemed to have trouble concentrating, so the counselor had suggested to Mr. and Mrs. Streeter that their daughter be tested for Attention Deficit Disorder. They had heard stories about their friends' children who were taking Ritalin, and believed that such a diagnosis would only lead to their daughter taking "habit-forming drugs." Neither Mr. nor Mrs. Streeter wanted their daughter relying on drugs and refused to have Beth tested.

As the school year was ending, the professional staff who worked with Beth would have to decide on her placement for the coming year, but the three people involved had not yet reached a consensus. Mary Grossi, a language arts teacher with over twenty-five years of experience, was convinced that the best thing for Beth would be another year in the third grade and Beth's language arts group was the least advanced of the five third-grade groups. Mary had said very forcefully in the last team meeting that "if this child goes into the fourth grade, she will be lost. She will not be able to read any of the textbooks and only will fall further behind." Mary had gone on to say, "During a second year in the third grade, Beth is likely to mature and to experience some academic success. Because it is her second time through the current curriculum, Beth is bound to have an advantage over the other students. If she can have some success, she will become more confident in her ability to do academic work." According to Mary, as a result of a second year in third grade, "Beth's self esteem will improve. Besides that, she just has not earned the right to go on to the fourth grade. Giving her a 'social promotion' will not be doing her a favor."

Brenda Anderson, the elementary guidance counselor, saw the situation differently. She believed that retaining the student would be harmful to Beth's self esteem. She cited research that indicated that retention did not prove helpful to students in most cases. For Brenda, the solution was to request that the parents provide a private tutor during the summer and when Beth began the fourth grade, a volunteer tutor could be found. Remediation, not retention, was the best answer for Beth.

Even Mr. and Mrs. Streeter did not agree on an appropriate course of action. They said that they could not afford a paid tutor during the summer, but thought it might be possible to find someone from the church who might work with Beth. Mr. Streeter supported retaining Beth in the third grade. He admitted that he had spent two years in the first grade and that the extra year had helped him to catch up with his classmates. Mr. Streeter had also been a high school athlete and had pointed out that an extra year of physical maturity would give Beth an advantage as a competitor.

His wife, however, disagreed. She thought that separating Beth from her grade-level friends would be devastating to her daughter. Socially and physically, she believed that Beth was more than ready to move on. If she repeated third grade, she would always be the oldest in the class and at graduation she would be almost nineteen years old. Mrs. Streeter believed that there had to be a better answer.

The person who had the primary responsibility for making a recommendation on Beth's placement for next year was her homeroom teacher, Nancy Park. Unlike her grade-level colleagues, Nancy had been teaching for only three years and had never recommended retention for any student. On the other hand, she had never dealt with a nonspecial education student who was doing as poorly as Beth. She remembered discussions about the value of retention in her college teacher education classes, and had her doubts about its value. At the same time, she agreed with Mary Grossi that Beth would have tremendous difficulty doing fourth-grade work. For Nancy, the decision was an agonizing one.

POSSIBLE DISCUSSION QUESTIONS

1. Is grade-level retention an educational option which should be considered in our schools?

2. What, if anything, should Nancy do prior to making her recommendation on retention?

3. What would you recommend, given the evidence available?

Case Study 7

A Mixed Blessing

Increasingly, school districts are hiring paraprofessionals, including a large number of teacher aides or assistants, to provide valuable assistance to overburdened teachers. Diverse student populations, which include special education students, can create a need for additional adults in the classroom. Although districts frequently prepare detailed job descriptions for these positions, the duties that the aides actually perform in the classroom vary widely. The experience and training of the classroom assistants can range from those who are fully certified teachers to others who have only a high school diploma. For a classroom teacher who has not been trained in the supervision and evaluation of adults, working with aides can be a major challenge. This is especially true if the teacher is supervising an older staff member.

Laura Santangelo was a formidable woman. She was almost six feet tall and could be very overpowering socially; she had been the first woman foreman in the local automobile assembly factory. Now retired, Laura had spent the previous three years volunteering in the school system and to the faculty, even among some students, she was known as the "Sergeant." No one, including the principal, wanted to upset Laura. Just a few weeks after she had retired from the factory, she had convinced the Board of Education that she should be allowed to organize a group of retired people to act as volunteers in the school and had done a marvelous job of recruiting an effective core of senior men and women. The volunteers worked in the office, the library, and made photocopies for the teachers. Others worked with grade-level teachers in the classroom and tutored individual students. With the exception of a few incidents, the program had worked very well and the faculty enjoyed having the help.

Laura herself had worked almost solely with the physical education teacher. Her drill sergeant manner was appreciated by the former Marine who taught physical education in the school. During the past summer, Laura's husband had passed away suddenly and, without his income, Laura began to worry about her financial situation. Superintendent Joan Lewis was a friend of Laura's and when her leading volunteer shared her financial worries, Joan suggested a solution. Given her long experience as a volunteer, she suggested that Laura apply for a paid position as a teacher's aide, and it surprised no one when she was appointed to the first available vacancy.

What did surprise some of the faculty was that Laura was assigned to Stephanie Meade's second-grade classroom. A twenty-three-year-old second-year teacher, Stephanie was a warm, quiet, petite young lady who truly loved her students. As a teacher and human being, one of her greatest strengths was her sensitivity toward others, especially children. She had not had an aide during her first year of teaching and was now assigned one because her class would include three students who had previously been in self-contained, special education classes. These children would pose difficult behavior management challenges and the special education committee had recommended that a strong aide be assigned to the classroom, in addition to a half-time special education teacher. When she first heard about the three students, Stephanie welcomed the challenge. She was confident that with love and care, she could help any child.

Although she had heard about Laura in the faculty room, Stephanie had never met her. When the assignment was announced, a friend on the faculty had offered Stephanie her condolences. Another teacher even suggested that she get used to saluting the sergeant. Stephanie merely laughed and said that she was sure that "they would get along just fine."

When they did meet, Stephanie came away from the encounter feeling that she had just experienced a hurricane. During their forty-five minutes together, Laura had done ninety percent of the talking. She explained that she knew these three children from physical education class and expressed her strong feeling that the only way to get them to behave was "not to give them an inch." She went on to tell Stephanie that "these kids need to know that you are watching them every minute. Sometimes they only listen when you raise your voice. Other times, the only thing you can do is grab them by the arm and move them." This last statement shocked Stephanie, as the only time she ever touched a student was to give him or her a hug. Laura had gone on to share her philosophy that it was essential that "the kids know who is boss in the class. The rules have to be clear and violators must quickly pay the consequences." Laura concluded by saying that she was sure that she and Stephanie would "run a tight ship."

During the meeting, Stephanie had tried to share her own philosophy that her class should "be like a loving family." As she told Laura, "Everyone needs to feel appreciated and loved. When there are problems in the classroom, we need to work together as a group to solve them." It appeared to Stephanie that Laura did not really understand this, because her next comment was that it was "unfortunate that corporal punishment was not allowed in this state, but whether or not you can spank them, these kids need to be afraid of you." Needless to say, the discussion had not brought about a meeting of the minds.

Stephanie went home that day and cried. She could not imagine being able to work with Laura. Everyone knew that Laura was a friend of the superintendent, and the principal and superintendent were more than aware that she herself was only a probationary teacher. What could she possibly do? Maybe she should just resign and look for a new position.

POSSIBLE DISCUSSION QUESTIONS

1. What are some of the considerations that should be discussed for any program using volunteers and teacher aides in the classroom?

2. Should the classroom teacher have the final say on a paraprofessional who is to be assigned to his or her classroom?

3. What should Stephanie do?

Case Study 8

Do I Want to Make
This Boy Ineligible?

> Academic eligibility policies can create difficult decisions for teachers. Instructors' judgment on a grade can be responsible for taking a student out of an interscholastic sport or some other extracurricular activity. Sometimes the teacher is sympathetic to a student who is having academic difficulties, but is torn by the need to maintain high academic standards for his or her class. Even the existence of an eligibility policy, especially at the middle school level, is a continuing source of debate among educators.

Dennis Ryan always read the answers to the essay questions first. Only after he had determined how many points a student had earned in the essays would he correct the multiple-choice questions. He would then add the points received on the objective questions to the points earned in the essays to establish the final grade. Despite the temptation, he tried not to second-guess his judgement on the essays. It was true that, at times, he had gone back and reread the essays to attempt to find justification for raising the student's test grade. He hated the subjectivity involved in grading essays and often felt that he was "playing God." Although Dennis knew that history called for subjective judgements by both historians and teachers of the subject, this did not reduce the amount of agonizing he did in trying to arrive at a fair grade for his students.

This problem was further aggravated by his school's new eligibility policy. With the added pressure on his urban middle school to raise the academic achievement of its inner city students, the faculty had devised a policy that stated that if a student was failing two subjects at the end of a grading period, that student would be ineligible to participate in athletics or other extracurricular activities during the next grading period. Of course, it was true that the student was entitled to a written warning halfway through the grading period. This being the first year of the policy, the middle school faculty had been very cautious and had sent out numerous notices after the first five weeks of school. Close to twenty-five percent of the students had received such warnings and now if they received two failing grades on their first quarter report card, they would automatically become ineligible for sports and activities during the next ten weeks.

Dennis could remember speaking out at the faculty meeting before the vote was taken on this proposed policy. He had commented that holding the right of participation over the students' heads as a bribe to stimulate achievement was not consistent with the school's philosophy. In his mind, the middle school should play a unique role in a young person's life helping to build self esteem. For Dennis, barring a student from an activity at which he or she could excel would only cause bitterness. This activity might be the primary reason that the student wanted to come to school, and it seemed to Dennis that taking it away for ten weeks would have a negative effect, rather than be a positive source of motivation. He had said to the faculty that "the purpose of our middle school should be to build up students and not tear them down."

He had been on the losing side in the debate, as other teachers had argued that extracurricular activities were a privilege to be earned, rather than a right. They thought it was inappropriate for a student who was not doing his or her work in the classroom to represent the school on the Student Council or on the basketball court. For these teachers, the primary objective of the school was to help students obtain knowledge that would allow them to lead happy and successful lives. After considerable lobbying by the principal, the eligibility policy had passed with approximately sixty percent of the faculty supporting it.

Shaking off the memory, Dennis began to look through the pile of papers he had been grading. He picked out the test paper of Tim Williams to reread it for the third time. Tim was over six feet tall and had been the high scorer on the seventh-grade basketball team last year. Given his size and physical ability, the coach had designated Tim as an "exceptional athlete," which allowed him to skip the eighth-grade program and play junior varsity basketball at the city high school. His skills were such that he would undoubtedly be in the starting lineup on the junior varsity team.

In the classroom, Tim had been failing for the entire first quarter and Dennis had sent home a warning slip after the first five weeks. If Tim failed social studies and one other course, he would not be allowed to play basketball for the first ten weeks of the sixteen-week season. Dennis's situation was made even more uncomfortable in that he already knew that the boy was going to receive a failing grade in English. Lorraine Lauer, Tim's English teacher, had informed him that there "wasn't any way the boy would pass English." Tim was reading at the fourth-grade level and his writing skills were atrocious. Even worse in Dennis's mind was the fact that Lorraine was not even convinced that Tim was trying. She had not needed to tell Dennis that the boy's written work was almost unreadable and that he made almost no effort on essay tests.

Having read many of the boy's papers, Dennis was quite aware of Tim's poor language arts skills. Still, in social studies class, the boy would sometimes come alive and participate effectively in classroom discussions. As a result, Dennis was sure that, as a student, Tim had the ability to do better work. His scores on the objective sections of exams showed that he was learning much of the factual material being taught.

After rereading the paper, Dennis recalculated the score and it again came up to sixty-three percent. The passing grade in the school was sixty-five percent. Dennis did not know in good conscience how he could add two points to the score. Still, he knew that if he did give Tim a passing grade, no one would ever know the difference and in fact, he expected the school administrators would be happier if the boy was eligible to play. All Dennis would have to do would be to give his young student two additional points on the essay section of the exam, and Tim would be able to begin his junior varsity basketball career next week.

Dennis knew that if he talked with some of his teaching colleagues, they would say that giving the boy points he didn't deserve would not in the long run be in the student's best interest. They might suggest that it would be better for Tim to learn early on that he had to keep his grades up; high school and college teachers were less likely to go out of their way to allow him to play basketball.

As he thought about the dilemma, Dennis reflected on the unique qualities of his young student. Tim was a moody adolescent who, on becoming ineligible to play, might well "crawl into his shell" and become embittered. It was possible that he would stop trying altogether. The clock was running and Dennis knew that he had to turn in his grades that afternoon.

POSSIBLE DISCUSSION QUESTIONS

1. Should schools have academic eligibility policies for middle school children?

2. If you feel such a policy would be appropriate, what form should it take?

3. What would you do if you were Dennis?

The Name Is Mr. Cole

First-year high school teachers are sometimes only four or five years older than some of their students. In such a situation, maintaining a proper teacher-student relationship can be a challenge. The students and teacher may have many common interests and occasionally may meet in social situations. Socializing with students outside the classroom, however innocent it might seem, can create unusual and sensitive situations for a young teacher.

Larry Cole had worried about taking a teaching position in his hometown high school. Unfortunately, positions had been somewhat scarce and when he graduated the previous May with a bachelor's degree in math education, he did not have a large number of alternatives. Having sent out numerous applications in the spring of his senior year, he had as an afterthought sent one to Newton Central School, where he had graduated four years earlier. Within a week he had received a call requesting that he come in for an interview. It seemed that his former high school math teacher was retiring and when the administration had checked with her, she had been enthusiastic about the possibility of having Larry be her replacement. Mrs. Clawson had been one of the reasons he had decided to enter a teacher education program. She had taught him math in both the eleventh and twelfth grades and he had come out of her classes loving the subject. In addition, Mrs. Clawson had been the senior class advisor and Larry had been class president. They had worked together during his senior year and had become quite close. Larry had even written to her several times as a college student to report his progress.

Larry had mixed emotions about going home to teach. He had looked forward to beginning his career in a new place. Also, his perfect job would hopefully offer him the opportunity to coach basketball, one of his major interests. Still, the interview with Dr. Lutz, his former superintendent, and Mrs. Kelley, the new high school principal, had gone extremely well. They had made him feel welcome and he was very much at ease talking with them. Their questions during the interview had been rather routine and none of them had been particularly difficult. Three days after the interview, Dr. Lutz called and offered Larry the job as the eleventh- and twelfth-grade math teacher. He would be teaching three eleventh-grade classes and two senior calculus classes. If he took the job, he would become the first student in the entire teacher education division of his college to be hired for next year. Accepting the position would also take a great deal of pressure off him about his future. This would allow him to really enjoy his final three months as a college student. Larry had asked for a couple of days to think over the offer.

He called his parents and they seemed delighted at the prospect of having their oldest son come home to work. His mother assured him that he could move back into his old bedroom, and as he would not have to pay an exorbitant rent, he could save some money. Next, he called Julie, who had been his steady girlfriend for the past two years. Although they had not talked about it seriously, he expected, or at least hoped, that someday they would be married. Julie was a nursing student who was one year behind him in school. The day he received the call, they had talked for hours and agreed that it was a great opportunity. As Julie pointed out, Newton was only twenty-five minutes away from the college and they could get together often. Larry had one other reservation about the job and that was that he had really wanted to take a position that also offered an opportunity to coach basketball. They decided that he should call Dr. Lutz to see if it was at all likely that he might have the opportunity to do some coaching. The next day, the superintendent called back and told him that he could coach the eighth grade boys' basketball team. Although he had been hoping for junior varsity, it seemed better than nothing and he decided that this was as close to the perfect offer as he was likely to get.

As they celebrated by going out to dinner, Julie and Larry had talked about some of the potential problems of teaching in his hometown. They had even joked about some of the situations he might encounter. How could he possibly call his former teachers by their first names? If he lived to be one hundred, he would never be able to call Mr. Jessup, his former English teacher, Norman. Would they even let him enter the faculty room? Julie even pointed out that those high school girls were really going to like their new math teacher. Although the seniors in his classes would have been eighth graders when he was a senior, Larry did know some of them from his church youth group. He also remembered that he was likely to have his cousins in class. As he prepared his lesson plans during the summer, these issues seemed very remote.

During his first week as a teacher, he had reason to recall his dinner conversation with Julie. The high school girls were very friendly, especially Carolyn Hooper, a student in his twelfth-grade calculus class. After the third day of class, Carolyn accepted Larry's offer to the entire class to stop by his room after school if they needed extra help with their homework. It now appeared that Carolyn was going to become a regular after school. Equally obvious was that she wanted to talk about issues other than math. She began to ask questions about his personal likes and dislikes and yesterday had asked him if he had a special girlfriend. As she was leaving, she asked Larry if he was going to chaperone the senior dance on Friday. He wasn't sure, but he was beginning to feel that Carolyn wasn't staying after school just to learn about calculus.

His twin cousins were also something of a problem. James, the extrovert, had entered his eleventh-grade math class with the greeting, "Hi, cuz." John, the introvert, had sat in class for a week and had not even acknowledged Larry. When asked a question in class, he merely said, "I don't know." On the other hand, James was always talking in class and it had reached the point where Larry was wondering how to deal with his loquacious relative.

One of the boys who he remembered from youth group had pointedly greeted Larry in the hall by saying, "How ya doing, Larry?" Without much forethought, Larry had responded by saying, "The name is Mr. Cole." The boy had moved on without saying anything further and Larry could not help but wonder if he had mishandled the situation. Other members of the youth group had been very friendly. In fact, the president of the organization had invited him to participate this Sunday in a coed touch football game on the high school practice field. Larry loved to play football, but was unsure whether as a young teacher he should be socializing with his students. Also, he was fairly certain that Carolyn would be participating in the game. With this growing number of problems, Larry was beginning to question the wisdom of the decision to come back to his hometown to teach.

POSSIBLE DISCUSSION QUESTIONS

1. Should teachers insist that students not call them by their first names?

2. What is the best way to deal with a student who may have a crush on the teacher?

3. What is the best way to deal with a family member who is assigned to your class?

4. Should Larry join the youth group for the touch football game?

Case Study 10

How Can I Make a Difference?

Whether or not schools should group students according to their academic abilities continues to be a source of debate. Frequently, there is pressure from parents of academically gifted students to give their children a more challenging curriculum. As a result, it is not unusual at the junior and senior level that the more ambitious and able students are given the opportunity to take Advanced Placement classes for college credit. With these students out of the mix, the remaining young people are those of more average ability. In many comprehensive schools, some of these students may be pursuing a vocational education program and are still required to take the basic subjects.

How does a teacher engage future tradespeople in the study of English literature? Do these students even need to read Chaucer and Shakespeare? Should an English class become a place where students work to perfect their writing and public speaking skills? How do you motivate young people to read books that seem to have no relevance to the rest of their education? Although the problem described in this case study involves high school students, teachers at every level face the challenge of trying to motivate their students.

Martin Gilbert was a first-year English teacher in the Lansing City School District. His large, comprehensive high school included students preparing for college, as well as some who attended a half-day vocational program. His twelfth-grade classes included students of various academic abilities. His favorite group was the Advanced Placement class, which is comprised of highly motivated students seeking college credit for the course. From the beginning, Martin had felt well prepared to teach this group, as he had just completed a master's degree in literature from an excellent liberal arts college. Each day, he looked forward to meeting with these students to discuss their assigned readings. Most often, the students came to class prepared and were eager to participate in the discussions. The three writing assignments he had thus far given had demonstrated that most of the students were proficient writers and he already sensed that he was building an excellent rapport with this group. Frequently, members of the class stopped by his classroom after school and they were always friendly when he saw them in the halls. Several of them had signed up to participate in the publication of a school literary journal. If Martin had been assigned five Advanced Placement classes, his job at Lansing City High School would have been perfect.

Even his so-called B groups, or middle level classes, were not a great problem for him. Certainly, the students lacked the intellectual spirit that characterized the advanced class, but at least most of them appeared to be trying. Some even showed a sincere interest in the work they were being asked to do. Still, Martin had to admit that in each of these three classes, there was a significant number of students who were merely going through the motions. The written work of these students showed little in the way of original thought, and in most cases, represented minimal effort. Many of these young people seemed more interested in extracurricular activities or their jobs outside of school. In any case, these classes were quite well behaved and at least at times responsive to his lessons.

It was Martin's C group that was the problem. These were primarily students who were in the vocational track preparing to be carpenters, auto mechanics, beauticians, and metal workers. Most seemed to place little value in the readings they were assigned and were unresponsive to his questions in class. When called upon, the students often responded by mumbling as few words as possible and the responses of two or three of the boys seemed almost hostile. Four or five of the students who did participate often seemed to be most interested in getting a laugh from their fellow students. On several occasions, Martin had had to caution students about using inappropriate language in the classroom. For the most part, the students just did not seem to take their reading and writing assignments seriously, and because Martin had only one set of anthologies to use for all of the groups, his latitude in selecting appropriate assignments was limited.

When he gave a writing assignment based on the literature, the students in the C group who did the work would hand in a few poorly written sentences. There were two students who seemed to be interested and appeared to try and Martin felt badly for them and expected that they were disappointed with the class. He tried to find ways to relate the stories and the poems to the interests of these students. Up to now, he had had limited success and had begun to realize that his own experience as a serious student in an academic high school and exclusive college had not prepared him to teach this group. Brought up in an affluent suburb, Martin found it hard to identify with city youth whose life experiences had been so different from his own.

John Lewis, the other twelfth-grade English teacher, had been on the faculty for almost fifteen years. When Martin asked him how to deal with this "slow group," John's response had been less than helpful. In fact, what he had said had upset Martin. John had said that the C groups were a "necessary evil." He went on to say, "You will never teach that group of animals to care about literature. Still, it is better not to pollute the other classes with these jokers. In my class, we talk about TV shows, sports, and maybe some current events. I try to be their friend. If they don't give me any grief, I make sure that they pass senior English."

Martin had thought about bringing his problem with the class to Mrs. Roca, the English department chair. By reputation, she was an excellent teacher who was respected by everyone in the school. She was also a formidable person who wielded great power within the building. As a first-year teacher, Martin knew that he was on probation. A proud young man, he did not relish the prospect of admitting that he was failing with one of his five classes. Mrs. Roca was a member of the interview committee and had insisted that he be hired. Martin really didn't want to disappoint her.

As a long-term solution, he had concluded that the grouping arrangement should be changed. Perhaps the Advanced Placement classes were necessary, but why couldn't the B and C groups be mixed? If that was not a solution, he wondered why different curriculums and materials could not be used. He felt too new to question a system that had been in place for so many years and he had not yet had the nerve to suggest a change. What he was certain of was that he had to find ways to motivate more students. Martin wanted to teach in the city, as the challenge appealed to his missionary zeal to help the less fortunate. These students needed teachers who were academically well qualified and who cared about them. He knew that there were teachers in this and every other city school who were making a positive difference. Still, after trying to teach the C group, he was beginning to wonder if he should update his resume and send it to the local suburban schools.

POSSIBLE DISCUSSION QUESTIONS

1. Do you believe we should be using "ability grouping" in our secondary schools?

2. What do you feel would be the best way to group students in a comprehensive urban high school?

3. Should all high school students be studying the same curriculum and using the same materials in a high school English class?

4. Suggest some approach that Martin might use to motivate his C group.

Case Study 11

The Halloween Party

Sometimes teachers have to make decisions on actions that could put them in a compromising position. In their efforts to do everything possible for their students, they must make choices that could involve legal issues. A degree of risk is unavoidable when teachers deal with students outside of the classroom. For instance, if a child needs a ride home after school or following a school event, should a teacher transport the student in a private car? Is it necessary that the teacher first gain permission of the parent? Would a written authorization be required? If the teacher were to have a written document, would it provide legal protection if there were an accident? Are there issues to be considered if teachers are to invite their students into a private home?

Jennifer Haley knew that the children in her special education class were not often invited to the parties of other children, and thought that having them come to her apartment for a Halloween party would be a wonderful experience. This would be their own party and she knew that they would be excited about the prospect of visiting her home. As their teacher, she had become very attached to these children and believed that they should have the same opportunity to socialize as their other peers.

She conceived of a Friday afternoon party, which would allow the students to go home after school to put on their costumes. They would then be driven the eight miles outside of town to the apartment where Jennifer lived with two other girls. Her roommates had agreed to help decorate and prepare the refreshments, and they had even volunteered to pick up the students and to bring them home.

Both of her friends worked in local businesses, but had visited Jennifer's classroom and knew and loved the children. The three friends had sat up until midnight the previous Sunday evening planning the event. First, Jennifer would read several Halloween stories, then they would play such games as pin the nose on the pumpkin, followed by the big activity, breaking a piñata filled with candy. They would then have a peanut hunt and end the party with wonderful refreshments. Not only would they have cider and doughnuts, but also there would be pizza and vegetables with dip. For dessert, the girls would make pumpkin cookies. All of the students would have their own party favors, which would include a small bag of Halloween candy.

When she mentioned the proposed social event to her friend and fellow teacher Shirley Teeter, Jennifer was given a word of caution. Shirley had told her, "Before you tell the kids about this party, you'd better check it out with Mr. Lundy." Deciding to take her friend's advice, Jennifer made an appointment with Principal Lundy the next day. At the meeting, Mr. Lundy pointed out some potential problems that caused her to question the wisdom of following through with the project.

First of all, the school system discouraged faculty from transporting students in private cars. Unless you were a specially trained driver using an inspected school vehicle, the practice was questionable. If an accident occurred, it could create a liability problem for both the employee and the school district. Assuming that there was no negligence by the driver, the school insurance policy would probably cover the staff member. This was especially true if the student was being transported to or from a school-sponsored activity. Mr. Lundy said he was unsure how the court would rule in such a case, but he was fairly certain the school insurance would not cover Jennifer's two roommates. He also raised the possibility of an accident during the party.

Before she left the meeting, Jennifer asked him about the advisability of having students take home a permission slip to be signed by their parents. Although Mr. Lundy said that it would be good to have the parents' written permission, such a document probably would not eliminate the responsibility of the teacher or the school if there were a problem. He also seemed very concerned about Mrs. Brumberg. A regular vocal attendee of Board of Education meetings, Amy Brumberg's mother had already begun two lawsuits against the school that questioned educational decisions made by administrators. Mrs. Brumberg was a vocal regular at Board of Education meetings. Jennifer had developed a fine relationship with Amy's mother, but it was evident that the principal was afraid of the outspoken parent. He had said, "If anything goes wrong with this party, we will never hear the end of it."

During the discussion, he had praised his young teacher for wanting to have the party. He had commented that, "it is clear that you want to do this because you care about your students. They are lucky to have a teacher who loves them." Even with his kind words, however, Jennifer could not shake the feeling that her principal was very nervous about her planned social event. He did not tell her not to do it, but neither did he give the idea his blessing. The principal's last words had been, "I am not going to be a principal who vetoes a party for children, but if I were you, I would think long and hard about the potential risks involved."

Janet, a fellow special education teacher, reacted strongly when she heard Jennifer's account of the meeting with the principal, saying, "Lundy is a weasel.

He won't give you clear permission to have the party because he is afraid to accept any responsibility. The man's terrified of that Brumberg lady. You want to do something for the kids and all he thinks about is the very remote possibility that something could go wrong." She went on to tell Jennifer, "He has no guts. If something happened, he would not be there to support you. You should get him to give you written permission or forget the whole idea. It is no wonder that teachers lose their idealism!"

Jennifer thought that Janet had been very hard on Mr. Lundy. She saw him as a nice man who just worried too much. Still, the conversation had given her serious reservations about the idea for a party.

POSSIBLE DISCUSSION QUESTIONS

1. Is it an acceptable practice for teachers to drive students in their private cars?

2. Under what circumstances would it be appropriate for a teacher to invite students into his or her home?

3. Should Jennifer go ahead with her plan for a Halloween party? If so, how should she do it?

Case Study 12

The Secret

At times, students choose to confide in their teachers. Sometimes the young person admires or trusts his or her teacher, and often the student feels more comfortable sharing a problem with a teacher than with his or her parents. To accept the confidences of a young person can place a teacher in a compromising position. In situations such as this case study presents, a decision may have to be made as to whether one should risk the trust of the student in order to protect the teacher's position within the school.

Lindsey Kozinski, an energetic first-year math teacher, looked even younger than her twenty-two years. In the high school cafeteria, she had initially been taken as a student and had only been charged the student price for lunch. After just eight months as a faculty member, however, she was already one of the most popular teachers in the school. She had been asked to chaperone at every dance and had been happy to do so. She sincerely enjoyed the opportunity of talking with her students in a social setting. As a former college cheerleader, Lindsey had been asked to be the advisor to the basketball cheerleading squad and had gotten to know the girls quite well. On the long bus rides home from away games, she had spent many hours listening to their problems. Although she had much in common with them, Lindsey had managed to maintain the proper relationship. The girls saw her as a successful professional whom they could and did respect. She did not confide in them about her own personal life, but rather had become an excellent listener. The junior and senior girls on the squad, of course, had their share of problems with boyfriends and with each other. Occasionally, there would also be stories about their disputes with their parents. Thus far in her short career, she had not had to deal with any particularly serious problems, but that had ended this afternoon when Kate Kelley had shared her problem with Lindsey.

Kate was a tremendously talented young lady. Along with cheerleading, she had been a starter on the soccer team, but her greatest talent was in music and drama. Last year, she had been a sensation when she played the part of Julie

34

Jordan in the musical *Carousel*. Not only did Kate have a wonderful stage presence, but she also had a superb singing voice. Just an average student in the classroom, Kate often seemed to lack confidence in social situations. She sparkled on the stage, but in real life she had little self-esteem. Her classmates found her to be somewhat remote and as a result, she didn't seem to have any particularly close friends. Even Lindsey had found it difficult to really get to know Kate.

Whatever her insecurities, Kate was an extremely hard worker in any activity in which she became involved. Lindsey really liked her and made every effort to be friendly and to take a personal interest in the girl's activities. She had been very enthusiastic when Kate told her that she had been chosen for the role of Guinivere in the spring production of *Camelot*. They had never been close, so Lindsey was somewhat surprised to see Kate come into her classroom after practice, where Lindsey had gone to pick up her briefcase. Kate asked if they could talk for a few minutes.

It was the day before a long weekend and Lindsey was planning to make the hundred-mile drive to visit her parents, but she saw that Kate was looking very unhappy. She put down her briefcase, sat down in a student desk and asked, "What's up, Kate?" After a pause, a tear appeared in Kate's eye and she blurted out, "I'm pregnant." Initially lost for words, Lindsey asked, "Do you want to tell me about it?" Kate responded that she really didn't want to discuss how it had happened, but she did want to talk about what to do. Even though she personally had never faced this issue, Lindsey knew that if she did, her first thought would be to talk to her mother and father. When she asked Kate if she had told her parents, the response was a vehement "no, and I don't want to." Kate went on to say, "My father would be humiliated and angry and he certainly would never forgive me. He thinks I'm the greatest thing that ever happened and both he and my mom would be ashamed and disappointed in their wonderful daughter."

Lindsey felt that she had to ask about the prospective father. Without hesitation, Kate let it be known that "the father is not someone I ever want to see again." At this point, Kate began to cry in earnest and had difficulty saying anything else. After taking the time to use some tissue that Lindsey provided, she said rather sheepishly, "Actually, I have been thinking about an abortion. This is my senior year, Miss Kozinski. I love cheerleading and it looks like our team might make it to the state tournament. You are not going to want a pregnant cheerleader out on the floor of the City War Memorial Arena." She went on to tell Lindsey, "Most of all, I am worried about the show. We have already begun rehearsals and by May I will be much too pregnant to be the beautiful Guinivere." It was obvious to Lindsey that Kate was seriously considering the option of an abortion, especially since she had already gotten the name of a doctor from Marcia Sterns, a girl in the senior class who had gotten an abortion the previous year. "Do you think it would be wrong for me to do this?" Kate had asked Lindsey. By now, Lindsey, too, was becoming upset and could not help but say, "Kate, I'm a twenty-two-year-old math teacher and I don't know what to tell you. What I am sure of is that you have to talk with your parents."

There was little conviction in her voice when Kate answered, "Okay, Miss Kozinski, I know you are right and I will tell them." With that, she had stood up and headed for the door as she commented, "Thanks for listening." Lindsey had sat in her room for the next ten minutes thinking about the discussion. She was sure she had not given the student what she had needed or wanted. Lindsey expected that she might well be the only person who knew about Kate's problem. What was her responsibility as a teacher? Lindsey was far from convinced that the girl would tell her parents. In fact, there was a real chance that she would pursue an abortion quickly. Lindsey thought about her own options. She could seek out Kate and try to continue the discussion, but even if she did that, she was not sure what she could say to the girl. She could call Mr. North, the principal, and ask his guidance. The only alternative she could see was to call Kate's parents. Lindsey knew that before she left for the weekend, something had to be done.

POSSIBLE DISCUSSION QUESTIONS

1. What should Lindsey do?

2. Does a teacher have a professional obligation of confidentiality when a student confides in him or her?

Case Study 13

I Don't Want One

Currently, there are significant funds available from federal, state, and local sources for purchasing computers to be used in the classroom. While communities might defeat some budget and building initiatives at the polls, they will often support bond issues to make computers available to students. Parents who have been forced to learn about technology on the job are especially anxious to ensure their children are computer literate. Except for the less affluent in our society, the number of students who have computers in their homes has been rising. For those children without access to computers at home, computer labs in schools are thought necessary to equalize educational opportunity. Sometimes the technology initiatives in school districts are thrust upon teachers who have not been prepared to effectively use the computers they are given. Occasionally, there are outspoken critics who suggest that the money being spent on technology could be used more effectively in other ways.

Don Owen knew that he was fighting a losing battle. There seemed to be overwhelming support for the Board of Education's decision to put $500,000 in next year's school budget to ensure that every classroom had at least one computer with Internet availability. The project would provide students access to both the school and local library catalogs, as well as make e-mail available to administrators and teachers.

An American history teacher with twenty-seven years in the district, Don did not support the decision. He felt strongly that if the district was going to raise additional money from the taxpayers, there were a number of more worthy programs to support. He remembered earlier projects that had placed televisions and VCRs in the classroom, innovations that were supposed to revolutionize education. In Don's view, one did not need technology to teach American history, and he felt most of his students through the years would agree.

A popular teacher who could hold the attention of a class with a riveting style, Don was without a doubt one of the most respected and loved members of the faculty. Students returning from college frequently stopped by his room to renew their acquaintance with their favorite teacher. The classroom itself was like a combination museum and library. Not only did he have hundreds of history books, but also numerous memorabilia. Along with his extensive collection of political campaign buttons and posters, there were pictures of all of the presidents arranged in chronological order. The classroom bulletin board, which student volunteers changed monthly, contained pictures and documents from the historical era being studied.

Most important to his success as a teacher was his style, which featured a keen sense of humor and the ability to create dramatic moments in the classroom. Personally, the students liked him, but it was his ability to bring history to life that made him a master teacher. All his life, he had read widely in his field and was always adding to his repertoire of human interest stories about people who had lived in the past. By supplementing the students' reading with his classroom presentations, he enable the juniors and seniors he taught to personally experience the color and richness of American history. Several dozen of his former students had been influenced by him enough to pursue careers as history teachers, and many of them tried to emulate Mr. Owens in their own classrooms. Normally a mild-mannered individual who stayed out of local and school political conflicts, he was now prepared to go to battle.

The Board of Education had scheduled a public meeting for that evening to answer questions about the proposed budget for next year. Administrators and board members would be making their case that spending half a million dollars on computers would greatly enhance educational progress. The plan to put computers in every classroom had originated with a member of the board and there had been little or no discussion with the faculty. Don had shared his concerns with other teachers, but most were either reluctant to become involved, or they agreed with Don. Several teachers had told him that they were anxious to have computers in their classrooms; one said she was looking forward to using e-mail to communicate with her grown children.

In any case, Don expected to be one of the few people who would speak against the expenditure. The representatives of the Taxpayers' League would be there and they, of course, would question any new, large appropriation in the proposed budget. Secretly, Don had a great deal of empathy with some of the group's senior citizens whose school taxes increased every year, even though their fixed pensions remained the same. Still, he knew that he would not endear himself to this group, either, as he was not going to suggest that the district should not spend any additional money at all. For years, he had advocated increased spending to lower class sizes and to increase expenditures for the school library.

In recent years, the number of district teachers had remained virtually the same, while the enrollment had increased by fifteen percent. As a result, elementary classes now averaged twenty-seven students per classroom and at the secondary level, the average class size was hovering around thirty. Don was convinced that with fewer students, he could do a better job engaging young people in discussions and helping them with their writing skills. With his five classes, he was now grading approximately 150 papers, rather than the 125 from five years before. After reading a number of research studies, he was convinced that lowering class size, especially in grades kindergarten through three, helped more than anything else to ensure students developed necessary reading skills. The $500,000 that was to be spent on computers could make it possible to hire new teachers. Don was convinced that these teachers would have a more positive impact on student achievement than placing a computer in every classroom.

Most of the teachers did not even know how they were going to use the new machines to benefit their students. Don's department chairman had told him about specialized software for history classes that would allow his students to engage in real life simulations. He had also argued that the Internet would be a valuable research tool for the weekly papers Don assigned to his students. On hearing this suggestion, Don had responded that "they do their research on their own time and it will not be done during my classes. Besides, they are going to get a whole lot of bad information and propaganda on the Internet."

Along with class size, his other pet project had always been to attempt to improve both the school library and his classroom library. He had spent thousands of dollars of his own money to develop the collection in his classroom, and this had proved invaluable whenever a student showed interest in a topic, as Dan could go to the classroom's book shelves and give the student some outstanding references. Unfortunately, there had never been enough money allotted in the budget for teachers to buy books for their classrooms. Several years ago, Don, along with the school librarian, had gone so far as to organize a Library Booster Club. The group had baked goods sales, car washes, and even a talent show to raise money for new library books. The first year, the organization had raised $4,000, but one year later, the district's budget for library books was reduced by $3,000. Members of the organization gradually became discouraged and after three years, the group ceased to exist. The problem, however, remained. Recently, one of his students had brought into class a library book that boldly predicted that "some day, the United States will put a man on the moon." Like many other books in the historical section, this book had been purchased in the 1950s. Despite inflation, the budget for library books never seemed to go up.

As he sat at his desk surrounded by research studies on class size, Don hoped to write a speech that would convince the board members that spending money to hire more teachers and buy more books would be a better choice than classroom computers. He was ready to tell the Board of Education, "I don't want one." A political conservative, Don knew that he would be seen by many as a fuddy-duddy who was afraid of the future. He was prepared to argue that there was no valid research to show that computers in high school classrooms would improve student learning. There were already two computer rooms in the school where students could go during their free periods and the library was equipped with computers as well. During his infrequent visits to the computer rooms, Don had noticed a significant number of students spending their free periods playing computer games. As an alternative, he was going to strongly recommend additional study and in-service training on the classroom use of computers.

This could be done at the same time that the additional money in the budget was used to reduce class size. He would share a study in the state of Tennessee that showed clearly that class size reductions in the primary school have a lasting influence on students. His remarks would also emphasize that the state of California, along with other states, was taking this research seriously and lowering its class sizes. Research was not as convincing for reductions at the secondary level, but Don knew in his heart that he could do a better job with fewer students. He could not support his arguments for library books with research, but Don loved books and he knew that many others agreed that computers should not replace them. In any case, after a couple of his favorite jokes, he was going to launch into a spirited speech at the meeting. For him, it was time to take a stand.

POSSIBLE DISCUSSION QUESTIONS

1. Do you agree with Don's position on the decision to spend the additional money on computers for the secondary school classrooms?

2. Prepare an outline of remarks that could be used either for supporting or opposing the $500,000 technology initiative in the budget.

3. What steps should be taken to introduce computers into the educational program of a school district?

Case Study 14

She Just Doesn't Support Teachers

In the area of classroom discipline, teachers feel the principal should support them. It is likely that more principals fail because they are perceived to be ineffective disciplinarians than for any other reason. Of course, when an administrator deals with a classroom discipline issue, the concerns of the student also have to be considered. In addition to teachers and students, parents frequently have strong feelings about disciplinary actions taken by the school. Therefore, a principal's methods of dealing with disruptive students will be judged not only by the teacher, but also by the community. An administrator who fails to maintain the respect of either the teachers or the parents can be in jeopardy. Sensitive teachers do understand the difficulty of the principal's role, and they are often forced to choose whether an administrator should be criticized or supported.

The meeting scheduled at the Presbyterian church had been organized by a group of concerned parents. The announced purpose of the session was to discuss school discipline at the Lakeside Elementary School. Approximately twenty-five parents had agreed to attend, and approximately half of the thirty-six members of the faculty had indicated their willingness to attend the meeting. When Stacey was invited, she had been noncommittal, and asked a fellow second-grade teacher whether Mrs. Pringle, the principal, was going to attend. Her friend paused and then told her that the people organizing the meeting didn't feel that it was appropriate to include Mrs. Pringle at this first meeting.

Dorothy Pringle was in her second year as principal at Lakeside. She was thirty-three years old and this was her first position as a school administrator. She had been a team leader in the sixth grade at a neighboring suburban school, and as part of her training for administrative certification, Dorothy had done a part-time internship in her own school. During her first few months as principal, she had made a positive impression, but criticism of her work had begun to grow this year and the number of critics was increasing. She was managing to upset a significant number of both parents and faculty members.

One of her major problems was that she was replacing an extremely popular administrator. Alice Reed had been principal at Lakeside for thirty-one years. She had helped to hire all but three of the present faculty. In the school and community alike, she was known and respected as an administrator who "ran a tight ship." Her method of enforcement of the school rules was both tough and consistent. At the beginning of each year, she had notified students and parents of the exact consequences for breaking each rule. If two children were found fighting in the hall, they both would be suspended for two days for breaking the rule about fighting. If students were late for school more than one time, they were placed on detention. It didn't matter if the sixth-grade girl was late because she was responsible for getting her younger brother and sister ready. Excuses didn't matter with Mrs. Reed.

Parents would complain occasionally about her discipline, but if the truth were known, many of them were afraid of the principal, especially those who remembered her imposing presence when they were in elementary school. It was also true that any student who went so far as to be sent to the office for disrupting a classroom could not even consider the possibility of a sympathetic ear when they were forced to face Mrs. Reed. Even when the teacher was obviously wrong in the way an incident had been handled, the principal would almost always find a reason to chastise and punish the child. It was rumored that early in her career as a principal, she had used the paddle to administer corporal punishment to disorderly students. The paddle had remained as a prominent decoration in the principal's office until her retirement. During her entire career, the teachers in the school were confident that just the threat of a trip to the office could often quiet a disruptive student.

Stacey Eckert had never met Mrs. Reed, but had certainly heard many tales about the retired principal. As a first-year teacher, she had been hired by Mrs. Pringle and from the beginning, the principal had been very nice to her. Although she was the only principal that Stacey had ever worked with as a new teacher, she admired the way Mrs. Pringle was always visible in the halls and classrooms. She was very friendly with the students and undoubtedly had a keen interest in the methods of instruction being used in the school. Stacey had already had two observations and conferences with the principal. The post-observation discussions and resulting reports had both increased her self-confidence and given her valuable suggestions for improving her teaching. Apparently, Mrs. Reed had seldom ventured into the classroom and certainly would not have done so without prior notice to the teacher. A number of the veteran teachers resented the new principal's habit of walking into the classroom and talking with students during an activity period. Neither did they always appreciate the sometimes lengthy classroom reports that Mrs. Pringle wrote after an observation. Even the smallest suggestion in these reports was taken by some teachers as a criticism. Mrs. Reed had never written anything but glowing reports for her tenured teachers.

Yet this sort of issue would not by itself have created major dissatisfaction with the principal. Those teachers who were really upset were concerned with school discipline and those who had been at Lakeside for a number of years talked frequently in the faculty room about how discipline had deteriorated. Several teachers had commented that "kids don't mind being sent to the office anymore." According to one teacher who had threatened to send Kelly Haines to the office, the student responded by saying, "Go ahead, Mrs. Pringle is a nice lady. She is nicer than you." The teacher went on to say, "I could have smacked the kid!" Another teacher had agreed that the mere threat of sending students to the office was no longer effective. At that point in the discussion, Stacey had interjected to tell her own story, which she now regretted. She shared the fact that this year, she had only sent two students to the office for being disruptive. In both cases, they were sent back to class within ten minutes with a note that the principal had spoken with them. At least in the second case, the child had acted worse after being in the office than before he had been sent. As a result of her comments in the faculty room, Stacey had received the invitation from a fellow teacher to attend the meeting at the church. She was encouraged to relate her experience at the meeting.

The parental criticisms of the principal were of a different sort. Mrs. Pringle's primary detractors were people who believed that her discipline had been too strict. Two boys who had brought knives to school had been suspended for five days. Their parents had argued that their boys had only wanted to show the hunting knives to their friends. Another five-day suspension had been meted out to a boy who had been caught lighting a match in the lab. One parent had complained to the superintendent about a suspension given when a child called an African-American classmate a "nigger." It was clear that there were certain offenses that Mrs. Pringle took seriously. A child who had thrown a paper airplane and hit the bus driver in the shoulder during the bus trip home had found himself suspended from the bus for a week. The parents had complained because they had to be late to work in order to bring him to school. All of these parents and a number of others would be at the meeting to protest the school's discipline policy. Stacey suspected that they, along with the teachers, would hearken back to the days when Mrs. Reed had been in charge.

There was no question that the two principals had different philosophies of discipline. Mrs. Pringle believed that for the most part, classroom teachers should solve their own discipline problems and should not be overly dependent on the principal. She had been quoted as saying that in her years as a classroom teacher, it had never been necessary to send a student to the office. Unlike Mrs. Reed, she always first listened to the student before taking any action on a disciplinary matter. While Mrs. Reed had a list of penalties for every infraction from which she seldom wavered, Mrs. Pringle tried to decide every case on its merits. As a result, she was sometimes charged with inconsistency in her enforcement of the rules. In the case of a fight, she was likely to first determine who had been the aggressor and give that child a strict penalty. If she concluded that the other combatant was merely engaging in self-defense, she might give that student no penalty. This change from Mrs. Reed's policy had created significant criticism for the new principal, and this practice of judging every case individually was causing some to feel that the principal had favorites. Stacey didn't believe these charges, but as a first-year teacher, she would have appreciated having someone like Mrs. Reed as the disciplinarian.

There was no question in Stacey's mind that the upcoming meeting on school discipline would be a session primarily devoted to criticism of Mrs. Pringle and that no one had even informed the principal about a meeting that concerned her own school. There was little question that one outcome of the group session would be a call for taking the problem to the superintendent, as well as the Board of Education, and Stacey wondered whether the group would even give Mrs. Pringle a chance to defend herself. Although Stacey was sure that her friends on the faculty would try to convince her to attend the meeting, she was not at all certain that it was the right decision.

POSSIBLE DISCUSSION QUESTIONS

1. Should Stacey tell Mrs. Pringle about the meeting?

2. Should Stacey attend the meeting?

3. If she does attend the meeting, should she attempt to defend the principal?

4. Should a principal have a rigid list of rules and consequences or should every case be judged on its merits?

Case Study 15

It's the Truth!

Student newspapers have sometimes created interesting problems for schools. The faculty advisors of these publications are often caught between an administration that is worried about the content of the newspaper and students who are protective of their right to free speech. Court decisions have helped to clarify the legal position of student publications, but the legal guidelines do not necessarily reduce the potential conflict. Although school authorities do have significant authority concerning the content of school newspapers, students can become outspoken in defending their belief that their work should be uncensored. In this case study, the faculty advisor is forced to attempt to maintain an appropriate balance between responsible journalism and the rights of a free press.

This year's student editors were the most outspoken and radical group Ben Lesley had ever worked with. After nine months as advisor of the monthly newspaper, *Scope,* at Bennington High, he thought that he had dealt with every kind of story the students might suggest. In the past, he had often been able to convince editors that their ideas might be all right for certain kinds of newspapers, but not for Bennington High's publication. He often had referred to his favorite newspaper, the *New York Times,* and its slogan, "All the news that's fit to print."

This year's group was led by the editor in chief, Tim Landers. After reading the book *All the President's Men,* Tim had decided that it was the role of the journalist to search out wrongdoing and to expose it. With this philosophy, it did not surprise Ben that his editor would write stories that were critical of the Board of Education, the superintendent, and the high school principal. Although other members of the editorial board of *Scope* might not have been as eager as Tim to become muckrakers, they usually supported his right to publish negative editorials. Ben had vetoed a number of Tim's submissions, but had allowed several that were mildly critical of school authorities. The one that may have caused the most discussion was a piece that compared school expenditures for the athletic program to what was spent on the school library, which ran under the headline, "Bats and Balls, but No Books at Bennington." Ben could not resist the alliteration in Tim's title and had approved the editorial. He had also let the students print an editorial questioning the principal's judgment in suspending five students for their inappropriate dress in school.

Although they had created no response from the administration, these stories had enlivened conversation in the faculty dining room. Even though most teachers supported the freedom being given to the *Scope* staff, there were some faculty members who thought the paper was going too far. One teacher had suggested that his colleagues would applaud the newspaper until they personally became a target.

Last month, Ben had said no to three of Tim's editorial ideas. After the third was turned down, the advisor had heard his student editor say to one of his friends, "Maybe we should just quit this newspaper and start our own underground paper. At least we could write what we wanted." Ben was not sure, but it might have been Tim's disappointment that caused him to approve the fourth idea for a lead editorial.

For some time, the principal and several members of the faculty were carrying on their own campaign to end what they saw as excessive expressions of affection by students in the halls. Students kissing or hugging in the halls would first receive a warning, and a second admonition would lead to a phone call to the parents of the two students. Additional violations of the excessive affection rule could lead to detention and possible suspension. The event that had led to the editorial occurred when two popular members of the senior class were taken to the office by a teacher for holding hands in the hall. The incident was soon common knowledge in the school, and Tim had written a deliciously satirical essay about the "love police." Although the teacher's name was not mentioned, the entire faculty and many students knew the identity of the enforcer.

The day after the paper was distributed, Ben was summoned to the principal's office. Jim Boyd, the principal, was retiring at the end of the year and he confided to Ben that the last thing he wanted was a public fracas on the freedom of the press. He shared the fact that Mr. Peabody, the teacher parodied in the column, had come to him and railed against "Ben Lesley's scandal sheet." Mr. Peabody said that he had been mortified by the editorial and that he had just been doing his job. The principal informed Ben that he had been told by both the board and the superintendent to do something about the "brazen way boys and girls are all over each other in the halls." One board member who witnessed a passionate kiss in the hall had termed the behavior "disgraceful," and had asked Jim indignantly, "What kind of place are you running here?"

Mr. Peabody agreed with the board member and had volunteered his services to help the principal "clean up the school." Jim had thanked him for the help and had commented that anything Mr. Peabody could do "would be greatly appreciated." When his eager teacher had brought the two students to the office for holding hands in the hall, Jim explained to Ben that he had felt compelled to support the teacher.

In any case, the principal explained, "Tim Landers and his cronies will have to stop printing this kind of editorial." The superintendent and a number of the faculty were concerned about who would be the next target. For that reason, Jim explained, he wanted to review every issue before it went to press. According to the principal, "If these stories don't stop, both of us will be in hot water. Whether or not you will be reappointed as advisor next year is already an open question with the superintendent."

Ben's initial reaction was anger. He had blurted out, "If you are going to censor every issue, there is no need for an advisor. What are we teaching these kids? The lesson will be that the 'establishment' just will not accept criticism." He went on to tell Jim, "You are just going to force them underground. What they are saying about their work is that they believe 'it's the truth!' Are we so thin-skinned that we can never be made fun of? It would be different if they were writing malicious garbage." He added, "Tim is potentially a great young writer. What we will do is embitter him against all authority if we censor the paper."

After Ben had calmed down, he realized that he was extremely sensitive because he thought the principal was questioning his judgment. Was it that lack of confidence that upset him or was he really worried about freedom of the press? In considering his dilemma, it seemed to Ben that he had only two alternatives. He could resign and leave the principal to find a more competent advisor, or accept the new procedure.

POSSIBLE DISCUSSION QUESTIONS

1. What do you think Ben should do? Why?

2. What do you think should be the guidelines for what can appear in a high school newspaper?

3. Do teachers owe their supervisors and employers support in issues such as this?

Case Study 16

It Just Costs Too Much

School districts vary significantly in the amount of money they have available to finance their educational programs or administrative operations. There is not only a large difference in salary schedules, but also in the funds that are budgeted for books, computers, and other supplies. Frequently, the biggest problems are experienced by city and rural schools. Jonathan Kozol has written convincingly about the inequities of public school financing, which is so dependent on local property tax. Affluent districts spend two or three times as much per student than less affluent districts located just a few miles away. At the same time, poorer districts frequently have more serious educational problems. Many of their students come from single parent homes with low incomes, and there are large numbers of special needs students, as well as an increased population of children whose primary language is not English. Teachers in these less affluent schools can be affected by the lack of necessary funding for equipment and supplies.

Julie Wood had wanted to teach in the city, and had requested a student teaching placement in a city elementary school. She had loved her experience at School Eleven and had really felt that she had made a difference with some of the children. On her last day as a student teacher, the class had held a party and many of the children had given her gifts. When she returned to her suburban college for the final semester, some members of her fourth-grade class had written her letters, and she had even returned to the school for the class picnic.

Despite the fact that Julie had been brought up in the suburbs, her student teaching had convinced her that she wanted to work in the city. She was thrilled when she was called to the downtown school district office for an interview. The combination of her excellent academic record, successful student teaching, and positive references were instrumental in advancing her candidacy. When the job offer finally came through, she accepted immediately. The salary of $28,000 per year seemed very exciting to a student who had never earned more than $6.50 an hour. She was somewhat surprised when she heard that several of her classmates who had taken jobs in the suburbs had salaries of $32,000 or $33,000.

The first thing Julie had to do was to find a place to live. She told her parents that she wanted to be fairly close to school so that she wouldn't have to drive through a lot of traffic each day to get to work. Besides that, she believed that if she was going to teach in the city, she should live there. When she and her parents began apartment hunting in the neighborhood near the school, her mother and father had quickly concluded that the neighborhood was not safe for their daughter, and Julie had to admit that she would not have felt comfortable living in that neighborhood.

A week later, the family returned to consider another neighborhood. Friends had told them that many young professional people had apartments in the museum district. Julie quickly fell in love with the many old, but well kept houses on the tree-lined streets. Not too far away were several blocks that had shops and restaurants where young people were sipping coffee at sidewalk tables. There were numerous joggers and in-line skaters on the sidewalks and it seemed that almost everyone they saw was under thirty years old. It did not take Julie long to decide that this was where she wanted to live, even if it did mean a twenty minute drive through the city to her school.

As they began to look at apartments, it was obvious that the rent was almost twice as much in the neighborhood they had visited the week before. Finally, Julie found a small, one-bedroom apartment that cost $600 per month plus utilities. Despite the seemingly high rent, she was thrilled with the apartment and signed the necessary papers. Soon, Julie and her mother were busy planning for the furniture, curtains, and other necessary items. While they were talking at the dinner table one evening, Julie's father had asked her, "What are you going to do about a car?"

One summer evening, Julie sat down with her parents to develop a budget for the coming year. The first draft of the budget seemed to work quite well, until her father reminded her of her college loans. Julie's dream of buying a new car was quickly discarded and with her father's help, she settled on a five-year-old Escort that already had traveled 60,000 miles. In any case, even with all of her living expenses, loan payments, and other expenditures, it seemed that she would be able to survive on her salary.

Julie's financial problems began to be evident midway through November. Every two-week pay period, it was clear that her expenditures were greater than her income. For the last few days before a paycheck, Julie was literally out of money and had trouble buying food and gasoline, and she was even staying home from church because she had no money to put in her pledge envelope. Somehow, the budget wasn't working. Julie knew what the problem was, but didn't really want to share it with her family.

When she had arrived in her second-grade classroom, Julie had found that there were almost no supplies. There only were a few used pencils of various sizes, six rulers, no colored paper or paste or even paper clips. Other than the textbooks, there was only a limited collection of books for students to read. When she asked the teacher next door about supplies, her colleague merely laughed and said, "Don't expect much from this district!" The principal told Julie that she would have a budget of $200 to buy supplies for her room. The district furnished copy paper, but everything else would have to come from her classroom budget. When she sat down with a number of supply catalogs, it quickly became clear to Julie that $200 would not come close to buying everything that she thought was necessary.

As classes began, her lack of supplies became increasingly evident, and several times during the first month, she had bought bags of classroom supplies from the Teacher's Pet store. She always spent a considerable amount of time in the large bookstores and on every visit, she found herself purchasing a new children's book for her classroom.

On the day after Thanksgiving, Julie decided that she had to speak to her parents about her inability to live according to the budget they had developed during the summer. After shuffling through the receipts and check stubs that Julie supplied, her dad looked up from his calculator and said, "Julie, do you realize that in three months, you have spent $247 at the Teacher's Pet store and at bookstores? These expenditures were not in your budget. What are you buying?" When Julie rather timidly tried to explain that she had been buying materials for her classroom, her father quickly suggested that she tell the principal that teachers should not have to buy pencils, crayons, and books for the students. He went on to say, "This should be done by the school district."

For the next several weeks, Julie tried to restrain her urge to buy additional materials. After ten days of good intentions, she decided that passing rulers back and forth between students was disrupting her lesson. She quickly forgot her resolve and went to the store to buy fifteen rulers, and while she was there, she bought some red and green colored paper for a holiday project. The next day, Julie asked in the faculty room about how other teachers dealt with the lack of materials. During the discussion, she had blurted out to her colleagues, "It's just costing too much!" One veteran teacher had explained that she had gone through the same problem during her first year. Finally, she said, her husband had told her that she should not "continue to subsidize the school district." She went on to say, "Now my class does not have colored paper or much of a classroom library. I feel badly, but on our salaries we cannot afford to spend hundreds of dollars each year on school supplies." Julie found the entire issue very depressing and thought about making an appointment with her principal to share her feelings.

POSSIBLE DISCUSSION QUESTIONS

1. What supplies do you feel the school district should make available to classroom teachers?

2. Do you expect you would spend your own money to supplement what was available in the school budget?

3. What do you think Julie should do?

Case Study 17

A Debate over Reorganizing Classes

Changing the way secondary schools schedule classes is one of the most popular innovations currently being implemented throughout the nation. Called block scheduling, this practice has almost as many variations as the number of schools who have adopted it. Schools that have yet to change their traditional schedules are sending representatives to conferences and on visitations to investigate the idea. At a time when schools are looking for ways to maximize the time spent on instruction as well as allow teachers additional flexibility, block scheduling has gained strong support in many communities. Yet almost every school district that has attempted to introduce the plan has seen opposition both from teachers and parents and the debate has often pitted one department in the school against another. Block scheduling has also caused conflict within a department, and individual teachers have had to make difficult choices.

Linda Gutierrez had been teaching Spanish at Sinclair High School for sixteen years. In recent years, the program had been especially strong and she was particularly proud of the fact that her new upper level Spanish class had twenty-five students. For her, this demonstrated that the students were interested in pursuing their study of Spanish; she felt that the vast majority took her classes seriously. As a teacher, Linda was pleased that a significant number of her students had continued their Spanish studies in college. Six of her former students were currently teaching Spanish and a number were working as interpreters. By any measure the school district used, her Spanish program was effective and any change that threatened the work she loved was a concern to her.

It seemed to Linda that the new idea of block scheduling would definitely change the way she taught. Currently, her classes met every day for forty-five minutes. She had developed a routine that allowed the class to move quickly through several activities each period, and this rapid pace and the variety seemed to keep the students involved and interested. For Linda at least, the forty-five minutes almost always passed quickly. Her lessons were carefully planned and

52

she was almost always able to review the previous days' work, introduce new material, and do a number of practice drills. In her advanced classes, Spanish was the only language spoken. The program contained a balance of speaking, reading and writing the language, grammar, and even some discussion of the Spanish culture. Students who had visited her as college students reported that they were much better prepared than their classmates. Linda and her students worked hard, but she was proud of the good results.

The block scheduling being debated by the faculty would change the pattern of five forty-five minute classes per week. Instead, Linda would meet with her students three days a week for eighty-five minutes. On the positive side, Linda calculated that her students would be in class thirty minutes more per week which, over an entire year, would mean 1,140 additional minutes. Thinking about what she could do with the extra time, it was obvious that it could make a positive difference.

On the other hand, she and her fellow teachers had some serious concerns about the change. First of all, she liked having her students five days a week. As far as the development of language skills, she believed that five days a week was preferable. The students needed daily practice and the new schedule would have some of her students going three consecutive days without speaking the language. Linda wondered how much they would lose over this extended time.

In order to increase instructional time, the new schedule would not include study halls. No one was quite sure what the impact of this change would be on students. Except for a thirty-minute lunch period, they would be in class all day. In addition, many faculty members worried whether there would be more students who just did not do homework with the new schedule. Many students were working over twenty hours a week outside of school and for them, the lack of study halls would have an adverse affect on the completion of assignments. Supporters of the new plan argued that with the longer period, much of the homework could be done during class. An added advantage would be that the teacher would be present to help the student. So often, if the student was in study hall or at home and had trouble with the assignment, he or she would merely give up.

Linda had tried to imagine how she would plan eighty-minute classes and doubted she could continue what she was presently doing for that length of time. Neither she nor the students could maintain the rapid pace for that long and even if she could, there would be a need for an increased variety of activity. If she merely gave the students thirty minutes at the end of class to do their homework, what had she really gained? Losing the daily repetition could outweigh the seeming advantage of the new schedule.

Across the faculty, teachers were having similar doubts. The music department was totally against the new schedule. Currently, the concert band and choir had rehearsals five days a week as part of the eight-period day. Under the new schedule, students would have to come in for rehearsals from 7:15 A.M. to 8:15 A.M., and the instructors were fearful that a significant number of students would drop out of the program rather than come to early rehearsals. The other alternative offered was to rehearse after school, and had this option been chosen, the athletes would have had to miss the first half of their team practice to be in band or choir. As the coaches would not look kindly on those students who chose to miss half of practice each day, the morning option seemed the better of two poor alternatives. Linda had heard that the department felt that imposing a 7:15 A.M. rehearsal was a violation of their contract and would challenge the plan. The supporters of the music program were not accepting this decision easily either, and the Music Boosters Club had already protested to the Board of Education.

The music teachers were not the only ones opposed to the proposed schedule. There were several outspoken critics in the math department. Like the language instructors, the math teachers felt that daily repetition in math was extremely helpful and worried that homework would become a thing of the past. Perhaps the most vocal opponent of the plan was Tim McCullough. He was the chairman of the mathematics department and had taught in the school for thirty-six years. Tim was known as a fine teacher, but also as a staunch conservative. In a faculty meeting debate on the block scheduling, he had reminded his fellow teachers of the late '60s and early '70s, when the school had implemented modular scheduling for three years. A supporter of the innovation at the time, Tim explained that "modular scheduling had been much more sophisticated and complex than the proposed block scheduling." The day had been divided up into twenty-minute modules and a class could be scheduled for any number of modules. He noted that "we had classes that met for 20, 40, 60, and 80 minutes. Every teacher was supposed to determine the ideal pattern for each of his or her classes. Time was not going to control us, we were going to control time."

He went on to say that after three years, the faculty had concluded that the scheduling had not really increased students' academic achievement. In his closing remarks, Tim had challenged the proponents of block scheduling to prove that it would really help students to learn. Although there were a number of articles being published, there was no major study that proved block scheduling would make a major difference. For Tim, it was just another swing in the education pendulum and he predicted that in a few years the school would be back to the forty-five minute period. He pointed out that it was similar to the method for giving grades. "When I came here, we used letter grades," he stated. "Then, we wanted to be more exact, so we went to numbers. Last year, we went back to letter grades."

Another opponent of the change, Cynthia Stanton, from the English department, had pointed out during the discussion that "if we really want to increase student learning, we need to add dramatically to the number of days each year we devote to school." She went on to say that the current 180-day calendar with its long vacations was a product of a time when the United States was an agricultural nation. The young people were needed at home during the summer months to work on the farm. Cynthia observed that, if anything, "we had reduced the number of days of instruction during recent years." This was illustrated by noting that schools were now allowed to deduct four conference days per year from the 180.

In addition to this deduction, there were half days for parent conferences and an increased number of hours and days for standardized testing. According to Cynthia, "What we really need is not to tinker with the schedule, but to increase the number of instructional days and be competitive with the rest of the world. In China, schools meet 251 days per year, in Japan, 220, and schools in Germany meet 219 days per year. What we should do is add at least thirty days. The block schedule is not the answer to our educational problems."

Others who spoke would be against almost any innovation. The Teachers' Union leadership objected to the way the administration had introduced the idea. The principal had established a faculty committee to study the concept and this group visited schools that were using the plan. Members of the committee, who had been personally selected by the principal, were going to recommend the new schedule for adoption at the next faculty meeting. The union leaders, however, felt the change would alter "working conditions," and the executive committee members were convinced that the administration should have negotiated the change with the union. If the schedule received a favorable vote, it was possible that a grievance would be filed.

The seven members of the Block Scheduling Committee and the principal had already made one major presentation to the faculty. They reported on the literature they had studied and also on what they had observed in their visitations to other schools. As the vote approached, everyone agreed that the outcome would be close.

POSSIBLE DISCUSSION QUESTIONS

1. What is the best process for a school to follow when considering an educational innovation such as block scheduling?

2. What departments in a secondary school might be most likely to support block scheduling?

3. Do you think that block scheduling is just another educational innovation which will come and go?

4. If you were Linda, would you vote for the proposed schedule?

Case Study 18

A Combat Zone

The conflict between the proponents of whole language and those who support an emphasis on phonics has divided educators during the past decade. More recently, the conflict has spread to the public arena and has become a political issue in some areas. At times, the debate has been harsh and unpleasant. Supporters of whole language have seen the advocates of phonics as having too narrow a view of the language arts. On the other side, those who emphasize phonics and the use of basal readers see whole language as an experimental scheme of the educational liberals. Even among education professors, there are major differences. As the decade ends, many are calling for educators to rise above this factionalism and incorporate the aspects of both methods. This is often easier said than done.

Lynnwood Elementary School had long had a laissez-faire attitude toward the methods teachers should use in reading instruction. While every teacher had a set of basal reading books, workbooks, and spelling books, in some classrooms, these materials seldom came out of the closet. Teachers had their own classroom libraries and collections of big books. Janice Prentice, who had retired as the school principal the previous June, had allowed teachers the latitude to teach language arts in the way they were the most comfortable. As a result, the faculty contained individuals on the far left who did not believe in the use of the reading series. They had long ago concluded that the stories in these books were poorly written and boring for children, and felt the workbooks and spelling books were even worse.

During the 1980s, the district had spent significant sums of money instructing elementary teachers in the whole language method. Five faculty members had spent a summer in New Zealand observing the program, and all of the district's teachers were exposed to approximately forty hours of in-service training. They also had a consultant in the district who demonstrated the new technique and worked one-on-one with teachers. A majority of the faculty was won over to the new approach, but there were still a significant number of holdouts.

Within a year, most of the skeptics had returned to the more traditional method of teaching that emphasized phonics. As a group, they were just as outspoken and committed to their methods as were the champions of whole language. During the years after the initial training, many of those faculty members who had been exposed to whole language left the district or retired. The new teachers who had been hired tended to be more moderate in their views and attempted to use the best of both methods. Since Mrs. Prentice had never raised the differences publicly, coexistence within the building was possible.

The end of the truce came a few months after the appointment of Bob Benedict as the new principal. At a faculty meeting, Bob announced that he was going to appoint a committee "to study our reading program and recommend to the faculty and the Board of Education a common, comprehensive, and effective plan for teaching reading in our school." In his comments to the faculty, the new principal had not taken a position on his personal views regarding reading education. After the announcement about the committee, speculation grew in the building as to who would be appointed. Bob asked for volunteers, but made it clear that he would appoint no more than seven individuals.

In February, Mary Lyon received a note in her mailbox that Bob would like to see her after school. Although Mary liked her new principal, she was a bit apprehensive when she read the note. A sixth-grade teacher with twenty-one years experience in the district, she was liked and respected by her colleagues and had a very positive reputation in the community. Although she had been through the whole language training twelve years earlier, she had settled on her own method for teaching reading. Mary liked to think that she had found an appropriate blend between the two approaches. Phonics certainly was taught, but she frequently used the big books and worked very hard to encourage her students to read outside of class. Her classroom had an extensive library that consisted of many books she had purchased herself. The students' writing assignments often came as a result of the books they were reading in class, and Mary attempted to teach grammar as a part of these lessons. For the most part, while she had abandoned the practice of giving students assignments out of the language arts workbook, she did give the students twenty spelling words to learn each week.

When Mary appeared in the principal's office, Bob began by telling her how much he enjoyed having her as part of the faculty. He noted that it "was obvious that her fellow teachers looked up to her." In addition, he noted that he had already heard in the community that "Mrs. Lyons is one of the best teachers you have." After this very complimentary introduction, he shared with Mary his purpose for the meeting. He wanted her to be the chair of the reading committee. Suggesting that she not give an answer immediately, Bob told her that he would check with her in a few days. To help her decide, he wanted to explain his strategy in formulating the group. His plan was to appoint two whole language supporters and two teachers who were in favor of emphasizing phonics. Along with Mary, he would appoint two young moderates who he hoped would help make compromise possible. His newest idea was to appoint four parents to what he was calling a "task force." These would be bright and articulate individuals who would help Mary find a "middle of the road" course.

As a teacher in the district, Mary had served on dozens of committees and a number of times she had been the chairperson. In fact, there had been a time when she had been urged to become an administrator, but Mary had quickly decided that she preferred working with children. Sitting around with adults in committees was not her favorite way to spend time, and when she was totally honest with herself, Mary knew that sometimes she was uncomfortable working on committees. This was especially true when there was conflict.

Knowing herself so well, she now wondered why she had agreed to accept the appointment as chair. Was she just flattered to be asked or had she lacked the nerve to say "no" to her new principal? He certainly had been nice and extremely persuasive. She liked to think that her decision was made out of a sense of duty to the school and, besides, she expected that she could do the job as well as anyone.

Mary had prepared carefully for the first meeting of the task force; an agenda had been prepared in advance and sent out to the members. Attached to the agenda was a written mission statement that she had asked Bob to prepare. In order to orient the new faculty members and parents in the group, Mary's first item on the agenda was a review of the recent history of reading instruction in the school. Going back a quarter of a century, she had reread the minutes from faculty and Board of Education meetings and taken notes on any discussions that related to reading instruction. She was hopeful that if she could put together a brief account of what had happened in the past, it would help the group put their present task in perspective.

Unfortunately, she did not even complete her ten-minute presentation before she was interrupted by one of the teachers. With the teacher's comments, the two camps began their warfare. It was obvious that the two whole language members had come prepared to argue their case and win over the moderates. Seeing that the whole language people were obviously taking the offensive, the phonics twosome went on the attack and Mary had to forcefully intervene in order to complete her historical account.

The second item on the agenda was to brainstorm as to the best way the task force could move toward its objective of establishing a "common, comprehensive, and effective plan for teaching reading in the school." At this point, the arguing began anew between those with extreme positions. Although Mary was their friend, the teachers seemed to ignore her efforts to maintain order. It was as if their feelings had been bottled up for years and they were now being given the opportunity to make their case. It was obvious that the parents were alarmed by the level of tension in the room, and although several of them attempted to join the discussion, as soon as they completed a sentence the two factions resumed their altercation. After forty-five minutes, which seemed to Mary like forty-five days, she interrupted the discussion and suggested that "perhaps we have done all that we can do today."

After the meeting, Mary felt as if she had just left a combat zone. She had not even attempted to set up another meeting of the group, and any confidence she had mustered regarding this assignment had been greatly depleted during the last hour. As a professional teacher, she knew that committee work was increasingly considered an important part of a teacher's job. Working with colleagues and parents was being hailed as the way to save our schools, but for Mary, it would be a blessing if the government or some leader would just impose a reading program. She knew that this was not going to happen and that she would still have to call another task force meeting.

POSSIBLE DISCUSSION QUESTIONS

1. Are we currently preparing teachers to play an effective role on site-based management committees? What, if anything, should colleges be doing to help teachers to be more skilled in this area?

2. What would be the best way for a district to establish a "common, comprehensive and effective reading program"?

3. What should Mary do about the task force?

Case Study 19

The Angry Parent

Teachers who try something new in their classrooms are often forced to defend their innovations. Parents and sometimes school administrators tend to think of school as they remember it as a child, and anything that varies from a person's conception of what school should be can create consternation and sometimes opposition for a teacher. Teachers must be prepared to justify undertaking an educational practice that varies from the norm. At times, critics can be very emotional and teachers must learn to deal with such reactions.

Jim Wood loved his classroom. For the past five years, he had been redesigning the room to allow him to teach in the way he felt most comfortable, and the final step had been the acquisition of ten new tables. For several years, he had been trying to convince Hank Flowers, the elementary principal, to replace the forty-year-old student desks that had been in the classroom since the school had opened.

Over the years, Jim had developed an aversion to students sitting in rows in his classroom and wanted to replace the desks with tables. Much of the classroom work was done in groups or hands-on lessons that required large surfaces. With four of the tables, he had established interest centers in the corners of the room along the wall. His math interest center had two computers, a box of calculators, rulers, triangles, and even an abacus. The materials in the science center changed frequently, so that if the class was studying geology, Jim would have his rock and mineral displays, and during a biology unit, there might be anything from leaves to a model of a human skeleton.

His social studies center now had a collection of local history artifacts that he had borrowed from the town museum. Finally, in the language arts center, there was an ample supply of children's books, appropriate age level periodicals and four comfortable chairs for reading. In the file cabinet was an individual writing folder for each student. On the walls of the classroom there were numerous specimens of student work, along with one large bulletin board that was changed frequently. As Jim surveyed his classroom, he had to admit that it was somewhat cluttered, but everyone who saw it agreed that it was the most interesting and exciting classroom in the school.

The plan for the room had gradually emerged in his mind during his first ten years of teaching. His student teaching experience had been in a very traditional school where the children were quiet unless they were recognized by the teacher and did not leave their seats without permission. He remembered that the classroom had been almost void of any visual stimulation, except for a few bulletin boards that stayed the same year after year. Even though he had learned about cooperative learning and other techniques in college, Jim began his teaching in very much the same way he had seen modeled during student teaching. The method was consistent with the way he had learned in elementary school and it seemed to be the approach that his new school expected.

As he looked back, he could not remember exactly when his thinking began to change. It might have been one of those numerous teacher conference days or more likely when he noticed that his students were not particularly happy in his class. Jim remembered thinking that both he and his students seemed to just be going through the motions. After trying a few science experiments in his class, he could not help but notice how his fifth-graders came alive. Sometimes, they came too alive. As he increased the number of group activities, there was no question that the noise level often increased. Still, he was convinced that the additional sound was, for the most part, students talking about what they were doing. Each semester, he added new cooperative education lessons, especially in social studies and science. Group projects that emphasized research increasingly replaced the traditional direct teaching method. When the classroom was connected to the Internet, many of the students sought to do their research "on the Net" and to use computers to complete their writing assignments.

The interest center idea was the result of a visit to a nearby elementary school. Jim had the students rotate between the interest centers most afternoons, and he was constantly searching for new ways to have students become actively involved in their learning. It was difficult for him to measure the success of his new approach, but he knew that he had frequent visits from other elementary teachers. It began with some of his colleagues stopping by and watching the students in the interest centers. During the past several years, delegates of teachers from other schools had also visited. What Jim was sure of was that the students seemed to like his new approach and the level of excitement and activity in his classroom continued to grow. Most significant to him were the frequent visits from his former students who seemed to like coming back to their old classroom. As Jim thought about himself and his profession, he knew that he was more relaxed and happy with his new style and that teaching was more fun.

Even with his many positive feelings, all was not perfect in Jim's class. Some students had difficulty adjusting to the freedom he allowed. As a result, Jim had resorted to a "time-out chair" where a student who was misbehaving would have to sit quietly for a designated period of time. For most of his children, a few minutes in the time-out chair would calm the student down so that he or she could then return to the activity. This form of discipline was not working with Billy VanBuren. The boy had spent significant amounts of time during the interest center period being disciplined, and Jim had thought several times of recommending to his parents that Billy be tested for Attention Deficit Disorder. After talking to the boy's fourth-grade teacher, Jim learned that the teacher had struggled all year with keeping Billy under control and that an evaluation had been suggested but the parents had refused. Yesterday at the beginning of a class science experiment, Billy had untied Mandy Pearce's hair ribbon and had run around the classroom using the ribbon as his tail. Upset with the behavior, Jim had put Billy in the time-out chair for the rest of the lesson.

That evening at home, he had received a call from Mr. VanBuren. After almost no introduction, the parent had said, "What is this about Billy being kept out of today's science experiment?" When Jim tried to explain about the ribbon, Mr. VanBuren interrupted him, saying that "apparently, Billy spends most of his day in the time-out chair. I have to tell you that the boy is convinced that you don't like him. He tells me that everyone else in the class is talking and you always yell at him. It sounds to me like that classroom of yours has no discipline."

After a brief explanation of his objective of getting students involved in learning, Jim was again interrupted by the parent. Hearkening back to his own days in elementary school, Mr. VanBuren shared his opinion that his son would be better off in a "more organized and better disciplined classroom." He went on to say that "Billy needs to be sitting at his own desk in a class where students speak only when called on by the teacher." Before he could continue, Jim intervened and suggested that Mr. VanBuren come in after school the next day to discuss the matter. The angry parent agreed, but closed the conversation by saying that he would be there, "but if I don't like what I hear, I am going straight down to Mr. Flowers' office and let him know what I think." Jim was never sure what his principal thought about his methods and expected he might soon find out. In the meantime, he needed to think what he was going to say to Mr. VanBuren.

POSSIBLE DISCUSSION QUESTIONS

1. Do you think that Jim developed a valid method for teaching his fifth graders?

2. Should he tell his principal in advance about "the angry parent?"

3. How should Jim deal with Mr. VanBuren?

Case Study 20

Transforming Education

For classroom teachers, the various reform initiatives in education can be a source of both confusion and frustration. From Washington, the teacher is told that "Goals 2000" should provide the vision for the future. Most likely, the government of his or her state also has a plan and of course every three or four years, there is a new superintendent of schools in the district with a new set of objectives.

When a teacher can find the time, there is a varied array of professional literature that focuses on innovations that are purported to have transformed education in one district or another. At conferences and workshops, there is always a new topic that is being highlighted. Any efforts to understand the forces affecting the profession are frequently undermined by the rigors of weekly and daily lesson plan preparation, as well as correcting papers. The conscientious teacher knows in his or her heart that despite all the conferences, books, and journal articles, what really matters is what the teacher and his or her colleagues do in the classroom each day.

After finishing the chapter, Ben put down the book and began to think about the mission of schools. He was reading a book of essays, edited by Evans Clinchy, entitled *Transforming Public Education* (Williston, Vt.: Teacher's College Press, 1997). The first section of the book outlines its purpose, which was "to raise some profound questions about the entire outcomes-based, standards-driven approach to school reform and the traditional hierarchical, authoritarian organizational structure that has for the past 100 years characterized—and, indeed, still characterizes—our present system of public education."

For Ben, the book had raised some very perplexing and difficult questions and the authors had caused him to reconsider much of what his state education department and school district were trying to accomplish. The primary focus of both was to raise dramatically the standards for all students and as a classroom teacher, he saw some obvious problems with this objective. He had underlined a section written by Linda Darling-Hammond that said, "The dramatic inequalities that currently exist in American schools cannot be addressed by pretending that mandating and measuring are the same thing as improving schools."

As a teacher in an urban school, he was very much aware of the inequalities in the schools of his state. As a graduate of a suburban district just thirty-five minutes from his present school, Ben could easily speak to the differences. The building in which he worked was over sixty-five years old and in poor repair. Ninety-three percent of the students were eligible for free and reduced lunches, and his five senior high school classes averaged thirty-one students. Few books had been added to the school library in recent years and there were only a handful of periodicals. There were less than twenty computers in the entire building.

The building class size and equipment were not the main problems he faced as a teacher. Most of his students came from dysfunctional homes and all of them lived in an unsafe and sometimes hostile neighborhood. He sometimes wondered if the people at the state capital who were creating these new standards and assessments really understood the problems in his school.

Most disturbing to Ben was the fact that the authors of the book were questioning whether the entire movement toward higher academic standards and universal testing were appropriate directions for our schools. He had been aware that there were different visions for the failure of public education, but he had never thought about the issue in a historical context. Linda Darling-Hammond captured for him the conflict in twentieth-century American education in a paragraph he had highlighted from the book:

> The criticisms of current education reformers—that our schools provide most children with an education that is too rigid, too passive, and too rote-oriented to produce learners who can think critically, synthesize and transform, experiment and create— are virtually identical to those of the Progressives at the turn of the century, in the 1930s, and again in the 1960s. Many current reforms were pursued in each of these eras: interdisciplinary curriculum; team teaching; cooperative learning; the use of projects, portfolios, and other "alternative assessments"; and a "thinking" curriculum aimed at developing higher-order performances and cognitive skills. Indeed, with the addition of a few computers, John Dewey's 1900 vision of the 20th-century ideal is virtually identical to current scenarios for 21st-century schools. These efforts, aimed at more child-centered teaching and more universal, high-quality education, were killed by underinvestment in teacher knowledge and school capacity. Lawrence Cremin argues that "Progressive education . . . demanded infinitely skilled teachers, and it failed because such teachers could not be recruited in specific numbers."

As a teacher, Ben was sympathetic with the current reformers' view that individual schools and teachers should be allowed more flexibility. Although the faculty in his school talked frequently about the need to "cover" the material in the syllabus, each year this became more difficult to do. Ben was aware that he had the same number of days for instruction but that there were now almost twenty more years to cover than when he began his teaching career in 1980. While he knew many of these events needed to be taught, the pressure to introduce the students to all of this information and to review it for a final exam had led Ben to lecture more and more.

When he had started teaching, he had been very enthusiastic about projects, debates, field trips, and student research, but because of the press of time and the ever present concern about the state test, his classroom method now most often would have to be described as direct teaching. He enjoyed the infrequent occasions when he talked with other faculty members about teaching styles, but too often when they did have time together, it was used to complain about what they perceived as unsolvable problems.

Sometimes, Ben thought about school as a factory and again thought about Dr. Hammond's words that "in one view, students are raw materials to be 'processed' by schools according to specifications defined by schedules, programs, courses, and exit tests. Teachers administer the procedures to the students assigned to them using the tools they are given: textbooks, curriculum guidelines, lists of objectives, course syllabi." Ben could see that his school was very much like this, and as he thought about the alternative vision of schools, he felt very supportive. Again, he turned to Dr. Hammond's essay to a section he had highlighted. The view she wrote about "underpins the new paradigm for school reform, starts from the assumptions that students are not standardized and teaching is not routine. Consonant with recent research on teaching and learning, this view acknowledges that effective teaching techniques will vary for students with different learning styles, differently developed intelligences, or at different stages of cognitive and psychological development; for different subject areas; and for different instructional goals. Far from following standardized instructional packages, teachers must base their judgments on knowledge of learning theory and pedagogy, of child development and cognition, and of curriculum and assessment. They must then connect this knowledge to the understandings, dispositions, and conceptions that individual students bring with them to the classroom."

This description appealed to Ben and he very much would have enjoyed the freedom to experiment and to really get to know his students. It had always been his goal to make his class an exciting place where students felt free to express themselves and to learn about subjects that were important to them. It was clear to him what he wanted to do, but he had to admit to himself that he didn't know how to meet the individual needs of the thirty-plus students he saw for an hour five times a week. The tools that he had brought to the profession from his days in a teacher education program were certainly inadequate. The only ideas he seemed to remember were Madeline Hunter's "elements of instruction," which were drilled into his head. In recent years, he had been introduced to Gardner's "theory of multiple intelligences," but no one had ever taught him how to use the information in a classroom. The same was true with the concept of learning styles. He knew that people learned in different ways, but this knowledge had not really affected the way he taught. The fact was that his classes in American history were almost identical to the way he had learned the subject in a suburban high school almost twenty-five years ago. He personally had enjoyed and had done well in his history courses, but he knew that this was not true of many other students.

The city school district had tried in recent years to introduce new ideas to the faculty. Most often it was done during a one day conference or in after-school in-service classes. Most of these experiences were short in duration and there had been little or no attempt to help teachers use the ideas in the classroom. He particularly remembered a stimulating session on authentic assessment. He had gotten several ideas from that workshop that he attempted to introduce into his program, but the lack of someone to talk to about his efforts had made it difficult.

Ben knew that he could do a better job in his classroom. He was also well aware that the reformers were right when they suggested that merely raising academic standards would not solve the problems in the schools of his state. It was clear to him that the academic success of the students was affected by poverty, broken homes, racial prejudice and drugs. These conditions were beyond the scope of the school to deal with alone. For him, it was very discouraging that a country with so much wealth could care so little about his students. Although his time was limited, he vowed to himself to become more politically active.

While he was attempting to affect politically the inequality of schools, he knew he would still have to teach his five history classes each day. There was no question that he received great satisfaction when his students did well on the state tests. At the same time, he was also aware that there was more to education than the ability to recall historical facts on an exam.

POSSIBLE DISCUSSION QUESTIONS

1. Do you feel that higher standards, additional assessment, and increased accountability are the correct prescription for the problems facing public education?

2. Do you agree with the reformers, who compare our current schools to factories where we are turning out students who lack creativity and critical thinking skills?

3. What, if anything, can Ben do to improve what he is doing in the classroom?

Case Study 21

Do They Really Mean It?

We have had enough violence in our schools to know that we must be vigilant. Fights, harassment, and students with weapons can be found in any school, and thousands of students and teachers are victims of a physical attack every year. Recognition of this problem can be seen in the fact that "Goals 2000" lists as one of its seven objectives that "schools will be free of drugs and violence." The "effective school research" that has so influenced recent school reform has also pointed out that schools must provide a "safe and orderly climate." Although there may be a higher level of risk in urban schools, we have recently seen examples of violence in affluent communities that were seen as being safe. It is not unusual for a teacher to be caught up in a situation where a judgment must be made as to whether a potential threat needs to be taken seriously.

Even though they were only eighth graders, Tim knew that the boys were capable of violent actions. He had broken up enough fights to know that when students became angry and upset enough, there could be serious injuries. As an experienced eighth-grade teacher, he had never before felt intimidated by any of his students, but the three boys who had just left his classroom had actually threatened him as they were going out the door. He had called to them to come back, but before he got across the room, they were out of sight.

It was the third week of school and the boys had yet to do a homework assignment. Although they had never challenged him openly in class, he had heard them conversing under their breaths to each other. As a result, he had purposely separated the boys during the two science labs he had done in class. Watching them, he had noticed that none of them had really participated with the other students in their group. They had merely stood apart with their arms folded. Several times, he had noticed them looking at their friends in the other groups. On the first unit test, two of the boys handed in blank papers and the third did very poorly.

Tim had talked to both the guidance counselor and several of the boys' current and past teachers. It seemed that midway through their seventh-grade year they had joined a gang. Tim had noticed that none of them ever came to class when they were not wearing their black gang jackets. None of the teachers were certain, but several were convinced that the boys were both using and selling drugs. From the assistant principal, Tim had learned that all three students had a history of suspensions and their offenses included disrespect of teachers, fighting, and harassment of other students. They had never been disciplined for drugs or bringing weapons into school, but the word among the students was that "these guys are bad news."

Several times, Nick, the smallest of the three, had shown interest in a classroom discussion, but had never really become involved in a meaningful way. It seemed to Tim that the boys were convinced that it was just "not cool" to show any interest in school. As a teacher, he prided himself on being able to communicate with almost any student, but his attempts to joke with these boys had failed, as did his efforts to talk about sports. Unlike most of his students, they didn't appear to be interested in talking about the city's professional football team. Once, he had even tried to use his limited knowledge of pop music to engage two of the boys in conversation. This, too, had failed.

This day, the students were again doing absolutely nothing in class, so in an attempt to break through the wall that had developed between them, Tim had ordered the students to stay after school. His hope was that if he could talk to them alone, he could perhaps get them to share why they seemed so antagonistic. When the three boys appeared halfway through the after-school period, they merely stood in front of Tim's desk with their arms folded. Even though he invited them to sit down and relax, they continued to stand. In his sitting position, Tim felt uncomfortable being below the eye level of the boys and decided to stand up to talk with them. From his height of 6' 4" he was able to look down on his three students, but they refused to look him in the eye.

As he spoke, the students seemed to be merely tolerating him and they were extremely unresponsive to his attempts to engage them in a conversation. The session seemed to be going very poorly and he could feel himself becoming frustrated. For some reason, these students apparently resented him. Tim, who thought of himself as a teacher who could find a way to make friends with any young person, began to feel angry. Were they trying to intimidate him? Anxious to deliver the message that "they were going to shape up in science class or be sorry," Tim, without thinking, was raising the level of his voice. He went on to lecture them, suggesting that "acting tough was not going to get them a high school diploma or a decent job." At that point, when Tim paused in his monologue, one of the boys said, "Can we go now?" Surprised, Tim merely said, "Yes, you can go, but I expect that from now on you will all come to class with your homework done and a more positive attitude."

It was when they reached the door that Judd, the tallest of the trio, said, "Mr. Sullivan, we want you to know that if you continue to hassle us, you will feel the consequences. For your own sake, we hope you understand what we are saying." With that, they were gone. As Tim recalled the scene, he was aware that there was an unquestionable level of intensity in the boy's voice when he made the threat. Was it possible that they would try to hurt him? Would they dare do something to his family? Is it possible that they meant it?

Tim's first thought was that he was overreacting. These students were only thirteen or fourteen years old. How could he possibly be a teacher if he was afraid of his students? In the past, he had always prided himself on the fact that he could handle his own discipline problems. He knew that his physical presence itself was almost always enough to ensure that his students behaved. Within the school, he was aware that he was thought of as a "tough teacher, but a really nice guy." In his seven years of teaching, Tim had never had to seek an administrator's help in the area of discipline. Why should he be worried about these three boys?

The thought crossed his mind that it would be helpful to share the circumstances of this incident with someone. He wouldn't tell his wife, Donna, as she already worried far too much about him working in an inner city school. He knew he could talk to one of his administrators, but somehow the thought of approaching them seemed a sign of weakness. He wondered if he was just trying to be too macho. Rather than talking to anyone else, he began to consider his alternatives for dealing with the situation. One option was to be proactive and call the boys' homes and either try to talk to them or their parents. He had not yet made any effort to learn about the parents, but his guess was that they had little or no control over their sons, even though that was an unfair assumption. Another way to deal with the problem would be to confront them in the morning and send them to the office before class. He could ask the assistant principal to keep them in in-school suspension until his free period. At that time, he and perhaps the administrator could try talking with them. This might be a prudent action, but he would have to get over the feeling that such an action would show that he was afraid of these young people. Would involving an administrator cause him to lose respect?

The other option was just to relax and take each day as it came. If the students were hostile the next day, he would deal with the problem when it occurred. In any case, Tim knew that he was feeling very uneasy about his situation. Was this what the teaching profession was coming to?

POSSIBLE DISCUSSION QUESTIONS

1. What do you think Tim should do?

2. What can schools and teachers do to minimize the danger of violence in their buildings?

Case Study 22

Are They Really Serious?

Many school districts struggle with potential or real financial crises annually. Since public schools are dependent on property taxes and state aid to survive, a problem with either income source can create a need to reduce spending, especially in communities that lack a strong tax base. Schools are also subject to political machinations at the state level, and at the local level, a change in the Board of Education membership can lead to reductions in spending. A recession in the national or in a state economy will almost always lead to a reduction in the state aid paid to school districts. All over the country, organizations committed to lowering property taxes are active, and sometimes representatives of these groups become prominent voices on a Board of Education. This is especially true if the community is experiencing an economic downturn. At such times, the potential budget cuts proposed can include long established areas of the curriculum. When such reductions are being considered, teachers must be prepared to defend their programs. Their jobs and careers may well be at stake.

Tony Pisceri was in his third year as an elementary music teacher in the city of Lakewood. He began students on band instruments in the fourth grade, and his fifth and sixth graders made up the Southeastern Elementary School Band. When the students left his school, they would continue in the junior high instrumental program. Tony loved his job, and so was concerned about the Board of Education meeting that evening, where there would be a discussion on possible budget cuts. Among those reductions being considered were both the elementary art and music programs.

The city of Lakewood was primarily a blue-collar community of 35,000 that was economically reliant on several large manufacturing facilities. During the past quarter of a century, the city had never been overly prosperous, but conditions had worsened in recent years. Each of the major factories had substantially reduced their work force and the overall population of the city continued to decline. Whole blocks of buildings within the city limits had been boarded up, real estate values had dropped in most neighborhoods, and middle class families were steadily moving to the suburbs or to rural villages in the area. Several of the major stores had closed during the past five years, but even with the economic decline, the city school district had managed to offer a better than average program for its students. This was due in large part to the commitment of the administrators, faculty, and staff. Salaries in the district were considered lower than those of the neighboring suburbs, and the average class size had crept up to nearly thirty students in grades K through twelve. Although the student population had decreased by ten percent during the past decade, the number of faculty had been reduced by over twenty percent. When a teacher retired or left the district, very often the position was not filled.

The crisis this year was brought on by the announcement three weeks ago that General Food, the second largest employer, would be closing its plant within six months and approximately 700 employees would lose their jobs. City officials predicted that the move would raise the unemployment figures in the city to somewhere between twelve and fifteen percent. Even more alarming to the school district was the fact that since the large plant would be completely closed down, the property tax paid by the company would be reduced by $300,000. This calculation, along with the news from the state capital that there would be a reduction in state aid, had caused a panic among Board of Education members.

A week after the announcement by General Food, the Board of Education had concluded that in order to maintain a stable tax rate, at least $750,000 would have to be cut from the forty-one-million-dollar school budget. Normal inflationary increases were going to create the need to increase most expenditures by 3 percent. The conclusion of the district's business manager had been that there would have to be reductions in personnel, and a list of potential cuts had been created at the last board meeting.

Clement Lawson, a retired General Food production worker, had been on the board for fourteen years. An outspoken representative of the local Taxpayer League, he had offered a number of suggested cuts. Of course, the one that alarmed Tony and his colleagues was Mr. Lawson's suggestion that the elementary art and music programs be eliminated. The board member had pointed out that state regulations did not require a certified music or art teacher at the elementary school and that instrumental music was totally a local option. When he made his proposal, Mr. Lawson suggested that "the classroom teachers could teach the children to draw and sing." As far as the instrumental program was concerned, he believed that it could start at the seventh grade. If parents wanted to begin their students with instruments earlier, they could pay for private lessons. Given financial realities, Mr. Lawson had commented that "by next year, we will be cutting the secondary instrumental program as well." He went on to say, "Besides, our high school band doesn't do anything anyway." The music teachers knew that he was referring to the fact that the band no longer marched in parades. The decision to end the marching program had occurred because increasingly students were unavailable for these special events. This fact had angered the veterans in the community because they no longer had a local marching musical unit for their Memorial Day celebration. In addition, there would no longer be a marching band to provide halftime shows at the Friday night football games. The band director had just given up trying to get students to commit to the extra time required to have a decent marching band. He refused to use his regular rehearsals to practice marching, and felt very strongly that students didn't learn anything about music parading up and down the field playing the same songs over and over. The decision had strongly damaged the reputation of the school instrumental program, and even though the three concerts each year were well received, most members of the community never heard or saw the band.

Tony knew that the art program was equally vulnerable. The district had a number of excellent art teachers, but too few people in the community were aware of the outstanding work the students were doing. There was an annual art show at the high school where student work from all the schools was displayed for two evenings. It was an impressive show, but it was usually attended only by a few faculty members and the parents of a small number of the students who were displaying work. Despite all of the preparation that went into the art show, the teachers, and probably the students, as well, were disappointed with the turnout.

The teachers in both the art and music departments were aware that a lack of community support could lead the Board of Education to seriously consider cutting or reducing their programs. Everyone remembered that there had been very little dissent several years ago when driver education and home economics were cut. All twenty-one district art and music teachers, concerned about their futures, had been present for a meeting after the potential cuts had been announced.

The meeting began with the chairperson of the music department recounting the discussion at the board meeting, followed by a young member of the art department asking the question that was on everyone's mind, "Are they really serious?" Although everyone at the meeting believed that there really was a possibility that his or her program would be affected by the budget crisis, the meeting did not result in any organized plan to respond to the threat. Most people seemed to think that the final result would be some partial reductions in the program. As it would be extremely uncomfortable if each department fought only for its own program, everyone agreed that the two departments should remain united in opposing the cuts.

Listening to the discussion, Tony was not convinced that a united front could be maintained. The group was unsure of whether their faculty union would take a defensive position during the board's discussion. The union would have to represent teachers affected by all of the cuts, and looking at the entire list, it was clear that many of the items would have a negative impact on not just music and art union members. For instance, there was a proposal to reduce the number of remedial reading teachers and another to cut back on the amount of time students spent in science labs.

One of the strong arguments that had come out of the art and music teachers' meeting was that elementary general music and art classes gave the classroom teachers their regular forty-five-minute break each day. Without this, the district would still have to provide supervision for the children while the teachers were given their required break from the students. Additional teacher aides to supervise students in a study hall could be hired, but this would not only reduce the savings from abolishing programs, but would be a questionable use of already limited instruction time as well.

Tony knew this argument could not be used for his instrumental music program. Although his students were out of class periodically for music lessons, it was not during a teacher break period, so by cutting the elementary instrumental program, the board would achieve 100 percent savings. Not only would the district save money on salaries, but money would also be saved on the purchase of music and certain instruments, such as tubas or most percussion instruments. These instruments belonged to the school district and often had to be repaired or replaced. There was little question that the district could save the most money by cutting the instrumental music program at the elementary school level.

As Tony thought about the upcoming board meeting, he knew he should be prepared to publicly defend instrumental music as a part of the elementary curriculum. He did not like to speak in large group settings, but it had to be done.

POSSIBLE DISCUSSION QUESTIONS

1. Prepare the outline of a speech that could be used to defend one of the following:

   a. The elementary art program
   b. The elementary general music program
   c. The elementary instrumental program
   d. Support for a reduction of one or more of these programs

2. What can teachers in the fields of art and music do to build community support?

3. Is this type of problem likely to become more or less frequent in the future?

Case Study 23

It's Just Too Much!

As instructional and assessments programs become more sophisticated, the amount of paperwork required of teachers has increased. These added responsibilities, along with the traditional progress reports and report cards, have added stress to teachers' lives. Much of this work must meet specific deadlines, and teachers at all levels are spending significant amounts of time outside of school trying to keep up. This work, on top of the ever present need to prepare various lesson plans and grade student assignments, has complicated the lives of many teachers. For those who teach special education students, there is the unique responsibility of preparing and tracking students' Individualized Education Plans. All of this work can cause personal problems for conscientious teachers.

Betty had to think of preparing something for dinner in a hurry. The faculty meeting had taken much longer than usual and her oldest son, Todd, had already asked, "What's for dinner, Mom?" If there was another jar of spaghetti sauce, she calculated that she could make a quick spaghetti dinner before her husband got home. An employee of a local electric company, Brian was in the third year of what would probably be a five-or six-year effort to complete a MBA degree at the local college. He was out two nights a week for class and a third evening each week he visited his aging parents.

During those three evenings when her husband was out, Betty spent till 8:15 P.M. with her sons, Kevin and Todd. Todd had begun kindergarten this year and Kevin was three years old. The boys were dropped off at a neighbor's house before school in the morning and Betty usually picked them up at 4:30 or 5:00 each afternoon. They were both very well behaved children, but right now they were hungry. With the water boiling for the spaghetti, Betty looked in the refrigerator for some lettuce to make a salad and found that it was turning brown. She was increasingly aware that the family diet was not as nutritionally well rounded as it should be. Although she had gone out and bought vitamin pills for the entire family, she knew that it was not the same as having real vegetables and fruits included in meals. If only she had more time, she would actually enjoy preparing more decent meals for her family.

Brian came in just as the water was boiling on the stove. Usually Betty was in control of herself, but with everything happening at once, she lost her temper. She was sputtering when he remarked, "I won't ask you how your day was." Betty was barely able to pause and smile for a split second to welcome Brian home with a quick kiss on the cheek. During dinner, after hearing about the boys' day, he asked, "Did it go any better today?" Betty responded by saying, "With the exception that I have my fourth cold this year and I was up till one in the morning doing report cards, it was great. Oh yes, and for the first time in my teaching career, I nodded off in the faculty room. During my free period, I was going to relax for just a few minutes. I was sitting in one of those comfortable chairs and before I knew it, Mary Lyon was waking me to let me know that the break was over. As a result, I have three hours of work tonight, rather than two."

With spaghetti still on his plate, Brian got up from the table and put on his coat to leave for his class, saying, "You ought to be done by the time I pull in and maybe then we can go out dancing." She smiled weakly and responded, "I'll be ready with my dancing shoes on." After he left, Betty was standing at the sink doing the dishes and thinking that she would really like to crawl into bed and sleep for a very long time. She wondered if it was just the late night yesterday, along with the cold, or whether she really was becoming run down. In the years before the children, she had jogged three or four miles most days, and even though she was a better than average player, she had only played tennis twice last year. The family bicycles that she and Brian had given each other two Christmases ago still looked brand new, as they had had very little use. Betty knew that she needed to eat better and exercise more, especially since she had gained ten to fifteen extra pounds since she and Brian had married seven years ago.

Just as she was finishing the dishes and preparing to play with the boys, the phone rang. It was Mabel Larson, president of Saint John's Episcopal Church women's organization. Betty's family attended church almost every Sunday and Betty attended the meetings of the group when her schedule permitted, which had only been about three times during the past year. Mrs. Larson called to ask Betty if she would become chair of a committee to plan and maintain a food kitchen at the church. She had said that the executive community had been unanimous in wanting Betty, a respected teacher in the community, to lead the program. Flattered by the request, Betty was also excited about the plan. She knew that their village had a significant number of people who could use the help, such as single mothers and senior citizens trying to make ends meet. For Betty, there was not a more worthwhile program that she could think of and she really wanted to accept the assignment. On the verge of saying "yes" to Mrs. Larson, she decided to take a day or two to think about the offer.

When the children were in bed, she sat at her desk and began to think about the time that would be required to lead the church project. Neither she nor any of the

other women knew very much about starting a food pantry. Along with the organizational and planning meetings, Betty expected there would be numerous hours
spent on the phone. She had led several committees and knew that this project
would be time consuming, but she didn't doubt that she could successfully lead
the group. Rather than simply writing checks for various causes, this would be a
chance to actually do something positive. Why was she hesitating? The answer to
that question was quite simple: she was already feeling overwhelmed with her job
and family, and Betty doubted whether she had the time and energy to take on the
leadership of the committee.

It was not teaching itself that was wearing her down, but rather the growing
amount of paperwork that went with the job. During the seven years that she had
been on the faculty, Betty had seen the workload increase. As a specialized
teacher, she knew there would always be Individualized Education Plans to do,
but the new reading and math programs now required her to record the progress
of each student regularly. Along with this, the school had adopted a mandatory
progress report to be sent to parents each five weeks between the issuance of
report cards.

Site based management had also added a new dimension to the teacher's role in
the school. Frequently, after school meetings stole precious time that faculty members had used for planning and grading papers. The blended or inclusion classrooms also required that teachers meet frequently during the school day for col-
lective planning. All of this had forced conscientious teachers to arrive earlier in
the morning and stay later in the afternoon. Even with this effort, most were taking work home almost every night and those teachers with families were nearly all
feeling additional stress. Although their spouses were helping out at home, many
teachers had partners like Brian, who had very active careers of their own.

Betty had often thought about being a stay-at-home mother and having more
time with the boys. Frequently, she had felt guilty about being away so much.
Since she had completed her master's degree and no longer attended summer
school, the summers had been less harried, but even now she spent many days in
August preparing for the new school year. Yet she would greatly miss her job as
a teacher; her closest friends were fellow faculty members and she truly loved her
students. Despite the added paperwork, she found the innovations which were
being introduced in her school challenging and exciting. Betty wondered if she
would be bored staying at home, especially after both boys were in school. Of
course, she could become involved in worthwhile projects, such as the food
pantry, but whenever Betty thought about the possibility of leaving teaching for
a time, the economics of the family quickly intruded.

With the house and car payments totaling over $1,500 each month, it did not
seem possible that the family could maintain its current style of living on one
salary. Summer vacations, family outings to movies and restaurants would have
to be severely restricted. The generous Christmas gifts to their extended families
would also have to be reconsidered. Most of all, Betty worried about saving

money to help pay for their sons' college educations and for retirement. As she opened her briefcase and took out the set of student papers to grade, she endeavored once again to put aside any decision about the future.

Try as she might, Betty could not concentrate on her schoolwork. Perhaps she could stop teaching and find a part-time job to supplement the family income. She also had thought about talking more to other teachers to find out if they, too, were having problems with the mountain of paperwork. Perhaps they could talk to their administrators and possibly even to the teachers' union. What if teachers were given extra free time during the school day for planning, participating on committees, and paperwork? She had heard that at one neighborhood school, special education teachers were given time off to work on the Individualized Education Plans. Even an hour each day would help reduce the workload. Determined to seek a solution beginning tomorrow, Betty put the ungraded papers back into her briefcase, and after checking on the boys, went to bed.

POSSIBLE DISCUSSION QUESTIONS

1. Do you think that what Betty is feeling is unusual?

2. What, if anything, can be done to help lighten the workload of teachers feeling the stress of their jobs?

Can't We Find a Compromise?

For the past two centuries, the primary elements in secondary school curriculums have been English, math, science, and history. It was not until the emergence of the social sciences as distinctive disciplines that history became social studies. As economist, sociologist, political scientist, geographer, and psychologist fought for inclusion in the school curriculum, what was once listed as history on the report card began to be called social studies. Heated discussions have been the rule in the twentieth century as historians have sought to maintain their principal position in the curriculum. In some areas, American history has become a topical review of the past with segments on politics in government, geography, sociology, and economics. More recently, there has been a debate between scholars, such as E. D. Hirsch, who believe that we need a uniform curriculum for all Americans that would include traditional history and literature, and those who have championed a multicultural approach to social studies. These teachers and scholars suggest that a primary goal should be to know about and celebrate our differences and to learn about other cultures along with our own. Hirsch, on the other hand, believes that the emphasis should be on a common cultural literacy that brings us together as a nation. These debates take place not only among scholars at the national and state levels, but also in individual schools where such decisions are often made.

Livingston High School, like many other schools in the state, did not have a regular social studies course at the twelfth-grade level. Afro-Asian studies were taught in the ninth grade, European studies in the tenth grade, and American history was required of eleventh graders. For years, the school's social studies department had sought to be allowed to offer electives to seniors. They were certain that, given the opportunity, a significant number of twelfth graders would choose a social studies elective. Most of the members of the department saw as the ultimate goal a requirement that all seniors take a social studies class. The state did not have such a mandate, however, and adding the requirement locally would require the allotment of extra money in the school budget. The Livingston administration and the Board of Education had never been willing to hire the extra teachers needed to offer twelfth-grade social studies.

Bob Byers, the new high school principal and a former social studies teacher, believed that it was inexcusable that seniors were not taking a social studies course. Midway through last year, his first in the district, he had told the social studies department that he was going to look for a way to remedy the situation. Just about a year later, he had announced that there was a way to at least begin offering an additional social studies class to seniors. After completing the master teacher schedule for next year, Bob realized that there was a teaching assignment each semester that would be open. He told the department chairperson that two social studies elective classes could be offered during the year. One class would be given each semester. Apologetically, he said, "It isn't much, but it is a step in the right direction." The principal had also noted that he would leave the choice of the electives to be offered to the department. He had said, "All you have to do is choose the electives and the guidance counselors and I will attempt to ensure that it will be possible for any interested students to take the courses."

Ben Ludlum, the chairperson, like almost every other member of the department, had strong feelings about what electives should be offered. The one person who did not have a preconceived idea on the question was Carol Newman. Carol thought of herself as an Asian-African specialist and taught ninth graders the required course in this area. She had no desire to teach anything else and no strong opinion on what should be offered at the twelfth grade level. When Ben had announced the possibility of the new electives, a heated debate had ensured. The chairperson asked that department members who were interested bring to the next meeting a brief description of an elective they would like to teach.

As the acting secretary of the department meeting, Carol had taken notes on the various proposals. As the only neutral, she knew full well that at the next meeting she would be asked to express an opinion. Looking at her informal notes, she knew that only two electives would be chosen from the six proposals. Before the meeting, she decided to reread the minutes:

POSSIBLE ELECTIVE COURSES

A. Cultural Geography
   1. Our students are not well versed in either United States or world geography. Many students cannot even locate their own nation's capital on the map.
   2. Our students have little or no understanding of how geography affects the cultures of various nations.
   3. Without a firm background in geography, our students will be at a great disadvantage in taking history courses at the college level.
B. Political Science (Civics)
   1. It is essential that high school graduates understand their own government.

2. Currently, state and local government is not included in any secondary school social studies curriculum.
3. Such a course could give students practical experience in observing and participating in local government. Attendance at public meetings in the community could be a required part of the course.
4. Too few of our high school graduates become active citizens and voters. They graduate uninformed and uninterested in public issues and despite the fact that they have the right to vote at age eighteen, many do not exercise it. This lack of knowledge and interest is dangerous for our democracy.

C. Economics
   1. Many of the political problems that face our nation, states, and communities are, in reality, economic issues.
   2. Nowhere in the first eleven grades do we teach basic economics. Students must know what is meant by the terms "fiscal" and "monetary policy." In addition, they should understand the workings of the market economy and be able to compare it with Socialism and Communism.
   3. Understanding of the Federal Reserve System and how governments can deal with inflation and recession is essential.
   4. Without this type of course, our students cannot be informed and intelligent citizens.

D. Consumer Economics
   1. What high school graduates really need to know is how to make a family budget, balance a checkbook, and fill out income tax forms.
   2. Students should be taught about the need to have health insurance and save for retirement.
   3. It is essential that our students, especially those not going to college, be taught to survive in our economically complex society.

E. Sociology
   1. This course is not only practical, but would be extra popular with students.
   2. The curriculum would allow discussion on topics that are important to young people. Beginning with the study of the family, the syllabus could include consideration of both racial and ethnic differences.
   3. A unit could be taught on the influence of the media and perhaps even the effect of religion on our society could be considered.
   4. Students could be assigned to do their own studies using polls or focus groups.
   5. Because it would include so much discussion about topics of interest, students would be "waiting in line" to take the course.

F. Psychology
   1. The first goal of education should be to help students better understand themselves and other people.
   2. In a psychology course, emphasis would be placed on human development so that the young people could better understand what they have experienced during their first seventeen years and what they could expect in the future.

3. The new concepts of "learning styles" and "multiple intelligences" would be included.
4. Young people could also learn about mental illness and be brought to the realization that like other sicknesses, it can be successfully treated. At an age when students are emotionally volatile and often depressed, this class could be helpful to them in their own lives.

After reviewing her notes, Carol realized that there were some excellent arguments for all of the proposed electives. She could not help but ask herself, "Can't we find a compromise?" If there was a way, she didn't know what it was. There were six proposals and only two could be accepted for next year. She knew that her colleagues would be seeking her support at the upcoming meeting.

POSSIBLE DISCUSSION QUESTIONS

1. Are you supportive of the current elementary and secondary standard curriculum in your state and local school district? How would you modify it?

2. If you were Carol, which two proposals would you support for twelfth-grade electives for the coming year? Why?

Case Study 25

To Refer or Not to Refer

In recent years, there has been an ongoing debate in the medical and educational communities over a condition known as Attention Deficit Disorder (ADD) or Attention Deficit Hyperactivity Disorder (ADHD). This problem is said to affect as many as five percent of American children and costs more than three billion dollars for special programs. Although there are a number of symptoms that educators and doctors use to identify such children, most often it is the inability to concentrate on educational tasks and disruptive behavior that cause a teacher to recommend referral of a student for diagnosis. Organized parent groups supporting additional educational services for ADD students are now found in many communities. Although drugs to control the behavior are available, they can have side effects, and some parents are unwilling to have their children take them. Since it is often the teacher who plays a major role in both the referral and diagnostic process, it is essential that all teachers be well informed about the disorder.

Nancy Bennett was in her second year as a third-grade teacher in the William Seward Elementary School. Working toward a master's degree in addition to teaching, she had been a very busy individual during her first year and a half as a teacher. With so little time, she had felt somewhat guilty about not having read many current educational publications, other than the textbooks she used for her graduate courses. Of course, she remembered learning about ADD during her undergraduate preparation and had even memorized the possible symptoms in preparation for an examination. It had been three years since she had taken the course and although she found the behaviors to watch for in her old textbook, she realized that the list was now ten years old. Yet using the characteristics in the book, she had reason to think that Johnny Oates was an excellent candidate for referral.

Nancy was considering whether or not she should raise the issue with Mr. and Mrs. Oates at their parent conference that was scheduled for the next day, but an Associated Press story in her local newspaper had shaken her confidence. The headline of the article read, "Diagnosis and Treatment of Attention Disorders Still

Uncertain" (*Batavia* [New York] *Daily News*, Nov. 20, 1998, p. 2). Referring to a committee selected by the National Institute of Health, the story questioned the diagnosis procedure currently being used. According to the article, the group of experts had said that "a consistent method for diagnosing and treating the disorder remains elusive." Chairperson of the panel, Dr. David Kupfor, a University of Pittsburgh psychiatry professor, was quoted as saying, "There is no current validated diagnostic test for the disorder." The article went on to suggest that committee members worried that doctors were too quick to prescribe Ritalin and other drugs. Dr. Kupfor was also quoted in the article as saying that "no studies have examined the effects on children who took the drugs for more than fourteen months." The more she read, the more Nancy was shaken by the article. It went on to quote another member of the group, Dr. Mark Vonnegut, a pediatrician, who said that "the diagnosis is a mess, but we all believe we are dealing with a severe problem." Another panel member reinforced the notion that there had been no studies to determine the long-term effects of the drugs.

The article had caused Nancy to rethink her tentative decision to recommend to Mr. and Mrs. Oates that Johnny see Dr. Pine, a local pediatrician who had treated a number of children in the school with the disorder. Mary Davis, the school nurse, had told Nancy that over thirty of the approximately 500 students in the elementary school were currently taking Ritalin or similar drugs. The school guidance counselor, who had serious reservations about these drugs, believed Dr. Pine was far too inclined to prescribe them. Even though Nancy, too, was concerned about the tendency to overprescribe drugs, she felt some kind of intervention was necessary for Johnny Oates.

Not only was the boy's educational progress unacceptable, but his habit of constantly leaving his seat and talking out of turn were disruptive to Nancy's class. She had tried several types of conventional motivation methods and behavior management, but Johnny would just not sit still and could only concentrate on a task for a short time. Although he was not overtly belligerent or aggressive, he did often bother his classmates. Rewards for good behavior might help for a short time, but Johnny would always revert to his undisciplined behavior. Even when he was assigned to the "time-out corner," he was consistently attempting to gain the attention of the teacher and his fellow students. When the class was working at their desks, he almost never completed the assigned task. During cooperative learning exercises, he sometimes annoyed his classmates with his hyperactive behavior. Twice when he had just refused to settle down, Nancy had sent him to the principal's office, and although on both occasions he cried the entire time he was there, the long term effect of the experience seemed to be nonexistent.

Nancy had consulted with the guidance counselor who suggested that she try to be extremely positive with the boy and praise him every time he did something right. Given his usual behavior, she had found it difficult to find many reasons to give Johnny positive reinforcement. The school psychologist, on the other hand, spent twenty minutes with Johnny and concluded that he should be referred to Dr. Pine. This advice was repeated after the psychologist had observed the boy in the classroom.

During a telephone conversation with Mrs. Oates, the boy's mother did acknowledge that Johnny was often "restless" at home, but that he did spend hours after school in active sports with the other children in the neighborhood. As a result of the conversation, Nancy knew that both parents were concerned about their son's lack of academic progress and were undoubtedly nervous about the report they would receive at the upcoming parent conference. There was little question in Nancy's mind that the parents would be hanging on her every word, so if she recommended that the boy see Dr. Pine, Mrs. Oates would be calling for an appointment the next day. On the other hand, she knew that if she did not make the suggestion, things probably would not change in her classroom. It seemed to her that the decision was extremely important because it could potentially have a long-range impact on all of her students. She concluded that her primary concern should be what was best for Johnny, not what was the most convenient for her as a classroom teacher.

Nancy knew there also was the possibility of referring the boy to the Committee on Special Education. If she did that, she would first have to inform the parents and in fact, the parents could be more upset if she sought to have the child classified as a special education student. Johnny had no obvious learning disability and had scored slightly above average on his IQ test. If she did suggest a special education review, Nancy was quite sure that the school psychologist would report to the committee his opinion that the boy should be evaluated for ADD. In the meantime, valuable time was lost.

In agonizing about her decision, Nancy was aware that doctors must make judgments every day based on the information at hand. Still, she was very nervous about being part of a decision that could have her student taking a drug that might in the long run be harmful to him. Even with these misgivings, she knew that Johnny had a problem that should not be ignored.

POSSIBLE DISCUSSION QUESTIONS

1. Do you believe that ADD and ADHD are definable medical problems?

2. Should students diagnosed with these disorders have the same program entitlements as those students judged to have disabilities under existing special education laws?

3. What should Nancy do about her student?

Case Study 26

We Just Want to Do It Our Way

Although it is an essential part of the preparation of any education major, student teaching experiences can vary greatly. For some, the period is the successful capstone of their training, while for others it is a time of discouragement and frustration. How well the experience proceeds often depends on the relationship between the student and the master teacher. Colleges preparing future teachers attempt to ensure that every master teacher who accepts a student is a fine model and an expert practitioner. Increasingly, those responsible for placing student teachers are finding it more difficult to find instructors who are willing to take on the responsibility for a student teacher. With the added pressure of preparing students for standardized tests, teachers are more reluctant to allow students to conduct their classes. Realizing that any student teacher could be incompetent, veteran teachers often prefer to keep their own class. Frequently, colleges must rely on building principals to help recruit master teachers. On occasion, some principals press a student teacher on a faculty member in need of some innovation. In any event, problems sometimes arise during the student teaching experience.

Bob and Tom had been friends since their freshman year and had taken Foundations of Education together during their first semester on campus. Throughout their course work, they had often talked about the possibility of student teaching together in the same high school. Now they had both been placed in a large suburban school located fifteen miles from the campus, and during the commutes they shared their experiences in the classroom.

That morning, Tom had said to Bob, "How come out of the nine student teachers in our school, you and I seem to be the only ones having trouble?" Bob had reminded him that Judy Tomody was also having some difficulties. Judy reported in their evening seminar back at the college that her master teacher began leaving her alone to teach all of the classes the third day of the experience. Up to now, she had received little or no feedback from her mentor, who seemed to be using Judy to provide her with the time to do her work as the president of the local teachers' union. Although it was only the third week of her assignment, Judy was teaching all of the classes and also doing lunchroom duty. Her master teacher would occasionally look in, but most often she was nowhere in sight. Although she repeatedly told Judy that she was doing a "good job," she had yet to say anything specific about her teaching.

Bob had commented that he would trade master teachers with Judy any time she wanted. His master teacher had hardly left the room and sometimes when Bob was teaching, he would join in the discussion. Even though it was his lesson, Bob still had not felt totally in charge in the classroom. He was not sure if the students were orderly because of his own teaching, or because Mr. Oswald was in the back of the room. As a result of this lack of independence, Bob still did not know what it felt like to be a real teacher. In fact, he believed that he had had more freedom in his Observation and Participation Experience during his sophomore year. At that time, he had actually developed and taught several creative lessons.

Beyond the fact that he was seldom alone, an even greater problem was that Mr. Oswald expected Bob to use the same techniques and lessons that he would have used. Every day, the organization of the class was the same. The period would begin with the request that students "take out your homework." It was then time to call on individuals to put the problems on the chalkboard. The teacher would then go over each problem with the class while the students corrected their papers. When this process was completed, the homework was collected. The teacher next introduced the new work while the students took notes. Practice problems were given while the teacher walked around the room to help. When these problems were completed, the teacher would then go over them on the board with the whole class. With a minute or two left in the period, the assignment for the next day would be given. Except for days when there was review or a test, the pattern was never altered.

During his junior year, Bob had had a math methods course that had introduced him to a variety of teaching techniques. These included such ideas as cooperative learning, using computer programs, and bringing in outside speakers to talk about how math was used in various occupations. He was very anxious to try something different, but had been discouraged by comments Mr. Oswald had made. The implication of his master teacher's remarks seemed to be that his own method was the fastest and most effective way to teach math. Like many other instructors, Mr. Oswald seemed to be very worried about the tests that his students would be taking in June. It seemed that for the master teacher, any deviation from "the method" would only mean wasting valuable time. This total reliance on the direct teaching method made Bob feel as if he were in a straitjacket.

Tom's student teaching problems were very different from those that were bothering his friend. His master teacher, Mrs. Kennedy, seemed to have almost no structure in her teaching. Taught in his education classes to organize the curriculum into units and daily lesson plans, it appeared to Tom that all Mrs. Kennedy did was assign the students a story or poem to read and they would all just talk about it the next day. Thus far, the only variation had been when the class read a play and parts were assigned. Watching Mrs. Kennedy, Tom thought that the students seemed to enjoy the class and his master teacher sometimes related the literature to problems that students were experiencing in their own lives. Still, most of the time in class seemed to be spent merely rehashing the plot of the story. When the class was over, Tom could not help but wonder what had been the point of the discussion. He knew that the master teacher's only lesson plan was to write in the plan book the name of the story, poem, or play.

When Tom had taught his first lesson on a short story, he had written out a three-page lesson plan that began with the objectives for the class. Mrs. Kennedy had quickly looked over the plan and said, "After a bit, you won't have to write all of this out. You will be like the rest of us and have your plans in your head." He had to admit that Mrs. Kennedy knew a great deal about the literature she was teaching. During the course of her lessons, she often shared interesting stories about the authors. It was the lack of any evident goals and structure in her teaching that bothered Tom. He had no idea if these wide-ranging discussions, or what seemed to him to be "bull sessions," were accomplishing any educational purpose.

In addition, he was bothered by the fact that in a two-and-a-half-week period, the students had only been assigned to write a one-page creative reaction to a poem the class had read. Although the students had some interesting interpretations, Tom was astounded by the number of grammatical errors in their work. If these students didn't improve their writing before graduation, they would all fail freshman composition in college. It was clear to him that unless they had the opportunity to write more frequently in their English class, they were not likely to improve.

As coeditor of his college newspaper, Tom had become a competent writer and he was eager to have a chance to help his students in this essential area. He knew, however, that the students would never complain about the lack of writing assignments and were happy with the informality of their English class. Mrs. Kennedy had a keen sense of humor and kept the atmosphere friendly and light. He remembered many of his college classes enjoyed a laugh on occasion, but there always seemed to be some academic rigor that pushed the students to reach for authentic meaning in the literature. In these classes, students were required to write often and their work was carefully evaluated by the professor. Students were not expected to make spelling or grammatical errors and when they did, it would affect their grade. Mrs. Kennedy, on the other hand, did not believe in marking up papers. She explained to Tom that all of those red marks only discouraged student writers. Instead, she would write a phrase or two at the end of the paper and had boasted to Tom that she could always find something good to say about every paper. To her credit, she would also try to make at least one suggestion for improvement on each paper. Tom had noticed that no matter how poorly written the papers were, every student received at least a B- and almost half of the class earned an A. He knew that when he finally did get to grade some papers, he would want to use the assignment to help improve the students' writing skills.

The boys had talked that morning about sharing their frustrations with Dr. Berry, who was working with both of them as their college supervisor. Each boy had already had one formal observation by Dr. Berry, and although he had given each of them several suggestions, his overall evaluation of their lessons had been very positive. They were quite sure that in the mind of their college supervisor, both of them were doing fine. While Dr. Berry seemed like a good man and they had enjoyed his visits, they hesitated sharing their problem with him. Several of their friends who had done their student teaching the previous year had given the boys some advice that had made an impression on them. They had been told to "always act as if everything is perfect. You should love the children and your master teacher. Do what you're told and do it with a smile. Your future depends on it."

When quizzed why it was important that everything appear to be so positive, their student mentor had reminded them that the most important references in their career placement files would be those of their master teachers and college supervisors. Any apparent problems during their internship in the schools could possibly appear in some form in these references. With jobs being scarce, anything that was less than a wildly enthusiastic tribute could be detrimental to a prospective teacher. The lesson seemed to be that no matter what, you should "grin and bear it." As far as the rest of the world is concerned, one must love everything about student teaching.

This advice caused both Tom and Bob to worry about doing anything at all about their situations. Up to now, all they had done was complain to each other, but both of them were feeling very disappointed thus far with their long-awaited student teaching experience. Tom summarized their disillusionment that morning when he said, "All we want is to do it our way."

POSSIBLE DISCUSSION QUESTIONS

1. What can colleges do to ensure that they provide a positive student teaching experience?

2. Describe what for you might be a perfect situation for student teaching.

3. What should Tom and Bob do about their situation?

Case Study 27

What Should We Be Teaching?

In the United States, the study of languages other than English is not often given a prominent place in our curriculum. Most school districts do not begin foreign language instruction until students reach middle school or high school. Some do make an effort to introduce other languages at the elementary level, but because most teachers in grades K through 6 are not fluent in another language, this is not common. Specialized teachers for languages in the elementary school are an added expense and hard to find.

For schools with foreign language, there can be disagreement as to where the emphasis should be placed in class. Some feel the school should concentrate on teaching practical vocabulary and oral communication. Others would argue that to learn a language correctly, students should spend a significant amount of time with grammar. Do students need to be taught to read a foreign language and is this more or less important than teaching how to speak it? Finally, in this age of multicultural education, should we be taking time to teach about the culture of the native country? The question becomes, "What should we be teaching?"

Middle School Principal Jack Sharpe had just completed his third observation of John Pearly, the seventh-grade French teacher in his school. This year, the principal had concentrated on visiting all of the tenured, veteran teachers in several selected departments. After each observation, the principal would have an extended conference with the teacher. Although Jack had been the school principal for twelve years, he knew that, in recent years, he had not spent sufficient time on instructional issues. His schedule had increasingly been filled with discipline and building maintenance issues. For the first time this year, he had an assistant principal and it was his hope, and that of the superintendent, that he would now have time to provide instructional leadership to the faculty.

Although Jack knew very little about the foreign-language curriculum, he had targeted this department because he had a sense there was some dissension among the three teachers who taught Spanish and French. His class observations and conferences with the three instructors made it clear to him that there was a problem. Not only did the language teachers seldom talk with each other, they also seemed to disagree on what the objectives should be for teaching foreign language in the middle school. Because it was a small department, there had never been a chairperson appointed and none of the three teachers had attempted to initiate any common planning.

With his observations complete, Jack knew that he had to bring the teachers together and attempt to create some sense of direction and unity. To prepare for the meeting, he decided to review his notes from the classroom observations. Rereading what he had written about Maria Lopez, it was clear that she was very much aware of the differences within the department. The youngest member of the department, she was frustrated with both of her colleagues. Spanish was Maria's native language and she loved to have the opportunity to speak it. As the eighth-grade teacher, she hoped that her students in their second year of Spanish would be able to understand her simple directions and carry on a simple conversation. During her first year at the school, she was shocked and disappointed with the small number of vocabulary words her students had learned in the seventh grade. Even the pronunciation of the words they had learned was very poor when they attempted to speak. When she spoke to them in Spanish, the students complained that they could not understand her. They reported that Mrs. Meyers, the seventh-grade teacher, had spoken primarily to them in English, which did not surprise Maria. When she had attempted to carry on a serious conversation in Spanish with Janet, she had asked her to "slow down." It was obvious to Maria that her colleague was not particularly fluent in the language.

Having studied Latin, Spanish, and French in college, Janet did understand a great deal about the structure of languages and the derivation of numerous words in modern languages. She had been exposed to the formal study of grammar in all three languages and was convinced that understanding the grammar and structure of any language would help improve students' skills in English. Janet felt that her role as a seventh-grade language teacher was to give students a solid background in verb tenses and other grammatical practices. With this base, they could go on to learn additional vocabulary and practice speaking the language in later grades. In her mind, if students were going to learn languages, they ought to be taught the basics first.

The other language taught at Middletown Middle School was French. There were twice as many Spanish students as there were French, so only one teacher was needed to teach both seventh and eighth grades. The current French teacher, John Pearly, had greatly increased the popularity of French, and the principal was concerned that the current program was not meeting the scheduling choices of some students.

John Pearly thought of language instruction as part of the larger goal of teaching children about other cultures. As a man who spent his vacations traveling, John had lived in France during each of the last two summers and loved everything French. As a bachelor, one of his joys was eating in French restaurants, visiting museums, and exploring the French countryside. John also had a passion for French art and had trays of slides not only of artworks, but also of various historic sites. Each spring, his middle school French class took a three-day field trip to Canada, which was always one of the highlights of his students' middle school years. This was not the only field trip they would take, as John always planned outings with his students to French restaurants and appropriate movies. In his mind, French class was much more than a place to learn a language. It was the opportunity for young people to celebrate another culture.

John and Maria enjoyed each other's company, and it was difficult for Maria to dislike such a happy and positive man. Still, she worried that his students were not learning French effectively and was concerned about their readiness for high school French. On the other hand, the students loved the slides and the field trips and some of her own students asked why their Spanish class did not have more slides and videos. There was also the concern that perhaps too many students were taking French just because of the trips and the other activities. Maria thought that this was unfortunate, because Spanish was a much more prevalent and perhaps more useful language for the students in her school district. It was also possible, she knew, that she was somewhat jealous of the popularity of John's classes. Of course, she could always blame her fellow Spanish teacher for the fact that many sixth graders chose French rather than Spanish.

For some time, Maria had thought about asking her two colleagues to meet and discuss the foreign language program in their school. As the junior member of the group, she worried that it might be thought presumptuous on her part to call such a meeting. Now, Mr. Sharpe was calling them together. After visiting their classes and talking with each of them, Maria was certain that the principal had determined that the foreign language program in his school lacked focus. Perhaps worse, he had also probably discovered that there was little or no communication among the faculty members.

Maria wondered if a meeting of the three before the session with Mr. Sharpe would be helpful. Perhaps they could clear the air and pave the way for accommodation at the meeting with the principal. If they were unable to work together, she knew that the principal would feel compelled to intervene, and given the fact that he had little or no background in foreign language education, it would be difficult to predict the results. Maria also knew that the principal was most comfortable and friendliest with Mr. Pearly. When she allowed herself to seriously consider their differences, she found something to value in the approaches of each of the department members. They really needed to get together and talk.

POSSIBLE DISCUSSION QUESTIONS

1. Do you think Maria should attempt to have a meeting prior to the session with the principal?

2. If such a meeting were to occur, what should be the purpose?

3. Given the three possible focuses outlined in this case—learning to speak the language, learning the grammar of the language, and the cultural approach — what do you think should be the major emphasis in a middle school foreign-language class?

Case Study 28

Whatever We Do,
Let's Make It Worthwhile

Almost anyone who thinks about public education would agree that teachers must continue to learn after their graduation from college. For decades, many districts have designated days in the school calendar for in-service training. Along with these one-day meetings, districts have paid their instructors additional salaries for attending classes outside of the regular school day. Although Boards of Education and faculty members recognize the need for this additional education, developing in-service programs for teachers is not a simple task. One major question is, who is going to decide the content of these offerings? For much of this century, conferences have been planned by school administrators, and the programs were often designed to meet specific objectives of the school district. At other times, inspirational speakers have been brought in to motivate the faculty. The conferences are often used to introduce teachers to new ideas in education, although many of these ideas unfortunately turn out to be merely fads. In any case, the programs are frequently criticized by teachers because they merely introduce an idea and do not allow for follow-up or guided practice. In recent years, committees of teachers have been empowered to help plan conference days and other in-service opportunities, but this involvement has not necessarily solved all of the problems associated with staff development.

Bill Davis was considered by his colleagues to be a bright and able professional. Within the community, he had a reputation as an outstanding chemistry teacher, and his principal and other district administrators saw him as a sensible and loyal faculty member. For all of these reasons, he was a natural choice to chair the first faculty in-service committee in the history of the Southwest Central School District. Prior to the plan for the committee, the administrative staff had had the primary responsibility for conference days and teacher in-service courses. Despite the fact that the Board of Education had been generous with funds for ongoing training for teachers, the evaluations given by faculty members of last year's offerings had been much more negative than positive. As a result, Burt Penn, the superintendent, had decided to let the faculty plan the program for the coming year. Working with the Executive Committee of the Teachers' Union, a highly representative group of teachers was chosen. Each school building had a committee member and both new and veteran faculty members were selected. The group was given a budget figure to finance the program with the sole stipulation that the final plan be approved by the superintendent and the Board of Education.

Bill knew that the committee had a major responsibility. This was undoubtedly the most dramatic gesture toward participatory management that Dr. Penn had allowed during his superintendency. Having served as the chief school officer in the district for nineteen years, he had not been a leader who had often shared power. Perhaps it was the frustration caused by the poor evaluations of previous programs or maybe he was changing his approach to management. In any case, if the committee failed in its effort to devise creditable offerings for the faculty, shared decision making would suffer a setback in the Southwest district.

After the first meeting of the committee, Bill went home wishing that someone else had been selected as chair. All eleven members seemed to have had their own personal agendas for staff development, and the discussion had been extended and, at times, heated. As he reviewed the minutes of the meeting, several themes seemed obvious. A significant number of high school teachers felt an express need to learn more about their subject areas, and one member had suggested that visiting scholars be invited to speak to the appropriate departments. Two nearby colleges could provide inexpensive speakers for almost every subject area, and the teachers thought it would be helpful if these scholars could meet with faculty members and share ideas from their disciplines.

The middle school teachers seemed to have less interest in subject area discussions. They wanted to hear from speakers who could talk about specific programs for middle school students. Counseling and mentoring programs were high on their list, along with the suggestion that there would be visitation days to successful middle schools.

Needless to say, the elementary teachers had their own ideas. Everything from "make and take workshops" to sessions on whole language was proposed. As Bill studied the suggestions made by the elementary teachers, he saw no real pattern. One thought that had been emphasized during the discussion was that if new teaching techniques were introduced, there needed to be significant follow-up and opportunities for guided practice. Along with the interest in teaching methods, there were several elementary teachers who had remarked how much they appreciated having well-known motivational speakers, especially for the fall conference. One teacher had said that "a good speaker can fire you up to do a better job and in our profession, we need that."

Given the wide array of proposals, Bill had decided that at the next meeting, the group would attempt to reach a consensus on the programs for the three conference days scheduled for the coming year. He thought that if he could get agreement on those programs, the group could calculate how much money would be left for additional offerings, but arriving at an agreement among the teachers of various grade levels would be difficult. In his mind, Bill was hoping that the committee could develop a theme for the year's conferences.

Several ideas had surfaced at the meeting. There were two teachers who were excited about the idea of authentic assessment, having heard an outstanding speaker at a recent conference. Another committee member had spoken about the possibility of focusing on recent brain research. This topic had sparked a heated exchange between two members of the committee. The proponent of learning more about the research suggested that "nothing was more important for teachers than understanding how people learn." A skeptic on the committee was adamant when he asserted that "the current research would not help any of them be better teachers." He went on to comment that "maybe years from now, there will be something practical." One of the elementary teachers was convinced that the district should concentrate next year on programs that would increase the self-esteem of students.

At this stage, Bill was sure that the group was not close to agreement on a theme for the year. He also knew that a decision designed to keep everyone happy would result in another year without an in-depth study of any topic. He was aware that the easy way out was to allot some time during the conference days for all of the committee members' pet subjects, but such a smorgasbord approach in the end would probably satisfy no one.

Looking at the minutes, he also saw reference to a suggestion made by the representative of the guidance department, who had suggested a series of days when teachers would visit industries and businesses in the community. The counselor had said to the group that "we could all do a better job if we could get out into the real world and find out what employees want us to emphasize in school." Another member had commented that visitation days were a good idea, but he thought that the faculty should be visiting other schools.

Bill had also thought of seeking input from school administrators, but discarded the thought when he concluded that they, too, would have their own agendas. At this point, he knew that administrators would support any plan that was designed to improve student achievement. The superintendent was very interested in computer training and Bill knew that it would have thrilled him to learn that the committee was spending its entire budget on learning to use computers as a teaching tool. There had been enough talk in the faculty room to convince Bill that a significant number of teachers did not share the superintendent's enthusiasm for technology.

As he considered the options, it was clear that he would have to find a way to reach a decision that could be supported by most of the faculty. Another thought that Bill had had was to send out a survey to all of the teachers. Hopefully, the results would point to some obvious options, but if the results were mixed, the situation might be even more confused.

There was yet another, totally different approach suggested at the meeting. One high school teacher had said that "maybe the time would be better spent if each building planned their own program for the conference days." Bill couldn't help but wonder if this was just an escape mechanism for the committee. Teachers were always complaining that they never had the opportunity to talk with their colleagues in other buildings. These conference days were about the only time that all district faculty members even saw each other. What if some schools decided to use the days for grade level or department meetings? Would this really meet the objective of in-service education?

Thinking about his dilemma, Bill could understand why the superintendent had been willing to form the committee. As he began to develop the agenda for the next committee meeting, he recalled the plea of a veteran teacher who had said at the end of the last meeting, "Whatever we do, let's make it worthwhile."

POSSIBLE DISCUSSION QUESTIONS

1. What is the best way for a school district to plan conference days and other in-service programs?

2. What should be the primary purpose of teacher conference days?

3. How should Bill go about reaching a consensus within the committee?

Case Study 29

Would You Just Talk to Them?

Sometimes children look to a teacher as the adult who they most trust. At a time when many families lack stability, a teacher can be the only consistent adult figure in a student's life. Faculty members who see children daily can be drawn into a child's personal life, and although they may want very much to help, they are unsure what actions are appropriate. Knowledge of the agencies and individuals available to help troubled young people is essential for any teacher, but even with this information, it is often difficult for a conscientious adult to avoid becoming personally involved.

Scott Foster had wanted to be a teacher for as long as he could remember. As the oldest of five children, Scott had assumed a major role in the family at age ten, following his father's death in an automobile accident. By the time he was sixteen, he was responsible for a multitude of household duties, including helping the younger children with homework and teaching them to play sports. While still a teenager, he had coached one of his younger brother's Little League baseball teams. His mother worked more than forty hours each week, so Scott cared for his younger siblings after school. Most children found it easy to talk with Scott, a sensitive and gentle young man, about any problems they might have as he was always empathetic and tried to do whatever he could to help. While he was a high school and college student, he had even on occasion called one of his brother's teachers to resolve a problem at school.

During his years in college, Scott had tutored individual children at a local elementary school and became a favorite of the children. Given his background, it was not surprising that when he became a fifth-grade teacher, many of his students looked to him as a very special person in their lives. Even when children tried his patience, he seemed to be able to see something good in every student. With Lenny Osgood, however, it took almost three months to establish any kind of a relationship.

The boy finally talked to Scott on the day before Thanksgiving vacation. Lenny was staying after school to help put up a Christmas bulletin board, which would welcome the students when they returned after Thanksgiving. All of the other children had left, but Lenny seemed in no hurry to go home. When Scott asked him about the upcoming holiday, it was clear that the boy was not looking forward to his time at home. After trying to get him to talk more about the problem, it became obvious to Scott that there were serious problems in the Osgood family.

During December, Lenny began to ask regularly if he could help Scott after school. Up to this point in the year, he had been a somewhat indifferent student and Scott thought it was a positive sign that he wanted to help out. Somewhat of a loner, Lenny participated very little in classroom discussions. When he was part of a group of students working on a project, he was most often on the fringes of the group. Scott began to observe him more closely and it became increasingly clear that Lenny had no close friends in the class, and kept to himself on the playground. Although he would do his homework assignments, it seemed to his teacher that he was merely going through the motions and was not performing academically near his potential. With an IQ above 120, the boy was barely doing C work.

In their after-school time together, Lenny slowly began to share shreds of information about his home life. The picture that was emerging was one of a marriage and family that was coming apart. An only child, Lenny was being pushed and pulled by both parents, who seemed to be incompatible. On several occasions, Lenny talked about his parents "yelling and screaming at each other." At other times, he confided that each parent had told him bad things about the other. Recently, his mother had said to him, "If Mommy ever leaves, it won't be because I don't love you." His father, on another occasion, had told him not to worry about the arguments because "your mother is just a little unbalanced right now." Lenny had asked Scott what unbalanced meant.

The boy's father was a salesman who was frequently away from home, and from listening to Lenny, it appeared to Scott that the boy's mother was often depressed. Scott also surmised that one or both of Lenny's parents might have a drinking problem. Worried that the parents might be physically abusive to the boy, Scott asked him if his parents ever spanked him when he misbehaved. There was no hesitation when Lenny responded by saying, "I don't do anything wrong and if I did, I don't think they would notice." In early December, the school had a parent's conference day, and Scott was hoping to better understand Lenny's situation when he met the boy's parents. Mrs. Osgood was scheduled to come in at 4:30 in the afternoon, but called the school at 4:15 and left a message that she was ill and that her husband was out of town. The next day, Scott called Lenny's home to try to reschedule the appointment.

In a very brief conversation, Mrs. Osgood said she would call and set up an appointment when she was feeling better. When he did not hear from her for a week, Scott called the Osgoods at home in the evening. Mr. Osgood answered and said that his wife was still sick and that he was leaving the next day for a business trip. As a way to end the conversation, Mr. Osgood promised to call for an appointment when he returned.

It was two days before Christmas vacation and once again, Lenny and Scott were working late in the classroom. Lenny seemed to want to talk and Scott decided to ask him how things were going at home. With that question, the boy quickly began a detailed account of a shouting match that had occurred between his parents the previous evening. Listening from his bedroom, Lenny had heard them talking about "a divorce." He heard his mother say, "Don't you even care about Lenny?" His father had answered, "I care about him as much as you do." Mrs. Osgood had then said that her husband really only cared about himself. The argument had gone on for a long time, and as he talked about the confrontation, Lenny began to cry. Scott put his arm on the boy's shoulder and told him not to worry. "What is going to become of me, Mr. Foster?" he asked. As Scott searched for an answer to the question, the boy blurted out, "Would you just talk to them?"

Scott had wanted to talk to the boy's parents, but he had not planned on an in-depth discussion on what was going on at home. He might have mentioned that Lenny seemed somewhat disturbed and distracted, but he had not expected to raise the family's problem. As a teacher, he was well aware that he had not been trained to be a counselor and as a young, single person, he certainly didn't feel qualified to act as a marriage counselor. Before he could respond to Lenny's request, the boy said, "They are both home now. Can you come home with me and talk to them?"

POSSIBLE DISCUSSION QUESTIONS

1. What should Scott do about the boy's request?

2. What is an appropriate role for a teacher when dealing with students' personal and family problems?

3. What are some possible sources of help for situations such as this one?

Case Study 30

Just Throw Out the Ball!

In this century, physical education has become a distinct class in school curriculums, and the design of these classes has been a constant source of debate among administrators and teachers. Some feel the goal should be to provide students a time during the day for strenuous activity to relieve the stress of sitting still in classrooms. Others view physical education as a way to prepare young people for a lifetime of physical activity, emphasizing instruction in such "lifetime sports" as tennis, cross-country skiing, jogging, and golf. Another approach attempts to fuse physical education with health education through classroom instruction in such topics as physiology, nutrition, and the benefits of exercise, along with physical activity. In the more traditional approach to physical education, students play team games, usually the same ones the school offers in their interscholastic athletic program. Thus, the physical education teacher who was also the basketball coach would probably offer an extensive basketball unit each year.

Along with the issue of what should be taught, physical educators have differed on the question of grading. Should there even be grades and should they be factored into the students' overall grade point average? How should a student be judged? Is it skill level or effort that should be weighed most heavily? What about physically handicapped students? Finally, there is the question of whether or not physical education classes should be coeducational. Despite the Title IX statute, are single sex classes more practical? Physical educators have varied opinions on all of these important questions.

Dennis O'Malley believed that he disagreed with his two colleagues on almost every professional issue they had ever discussed. Having just completed his master's degree in physical education, he had been introduced to the current literature in his field, and three nights a week for the past two years he had heard his professors criticizing the "just throw out the ball" approach to physical education. The instructors were referring to gym teachers who were also basketball coaches, and who had their students learning about and playing basketball for weeks on end. Other teachers would have the children play soccer in the fall, basketball and volleyball during the winter, and softball in the spring.

Instead of this traditional approach to physical education classes, Dennis had been learning about the importance of proper warm-up before exercising and the need to offer a variety of physical activities. For his college teachers, team sports were much less important than physical activities that students could use throughout their lives. They felt students should be instructed on the importance of physical activity for overall health, emphasizing the need for aerobic conditioning and healthy lifestyles including proper nutrition and the avoidance of alcohol and other drugs. His teachers suggested that videotapes and classroom demonstrations should be considered an essential part of physical education classes. In his coursework, the importance of the physical education teacher as a model for young people was also stressed. An overweight teacher who smoked and drank was sending the wrong message to his or her students. Overall, his graduate study had succeeded in making Dennis a man with a mission.

He believed strongly that physical education teachers could make a difference in helping their students adopt a healthy lifestyle. Both of his colleagues in the department had a different emphasis in their teaching. To begin with, Dennis believed that both teachers were more interested in coaching than in their classes. Bob Boyd had been the boys' basketball coach for seventeen years and had had two state champion teams. A frequent winner of the Coach of the Year Award, Bob was a much admired member of the community who had established a Saturday morning league for elementary school boys and a Basketball Booster Club, which raised money to send the players to well-known summer basketball camps. Both his enduring interest in the sport and his desire to build his team had resulted in Bob spending up to ten weeks a year concentrating on basketball in his physical education classes.

Molly Lewin, although not as successful as Bob, was also a coach and had been attempting to build a strong girls' volleyball program for many years. Lacking the personal charisma and political skills of Bob, she had had only limited success with her teams. In her mind, the reason was that the school district favored boys' sports. She was unhappy both with her longtime colleague and the school administration. Although she had attempted to establish an elementary girls' volleyball program similar to the boys' program, she was frustrated that it never was included in the budget. She knew that Bob had told the administration that elementary students were too young to play volleyball and that the middle school was a better time to introduce the sport.

Although both of his colleagues were cordial to Dennis, he knew that both saw him as a young, naive idealist. They had urged him to consider coaching varsity baseball when the position was vacant, but he had decided to stay with his middle school coaching position. For him, teaching the fundamentals of a game was more fun than worrying about winning and losing. It was also true that for Dennis, coaching remained a secondary activity that was less important to him than his physical education classes. In fact, he liked to think of his coaching as an extension of his classes.

The difference in philosophy had now become an important factor as the department was being asked to reevaluate its program. The state had adopted a list of educational standards that dealt with every phase of the curriculum. As a result, the superintendent had required each department to put in writing how they proposed to meet the new requirements. The primary standard adopted for physical education was that schools should "ensure that all students are instructed in the importance of physical activity for a healthy lifestyle." When the three members of the department had recently met, Dennis' two colleagues had suggested that he "write something up for the superintendent. . . . You're the scholar." Dennis, however, was determined to do more than just write a paragraph and was preparing a K through 12 physical education curriculum for the entire district that would probably come as a shock to both Bob and Molly.

While he was working on this document, a ruling was published from the State Education Department that caused immediate conflict within the department. The ruling allowed school districts to excuse students who were participating in interscholastic sports from physical education classes for the duration of that sport's season. The rationale was that since these students were exercising ten to twelve hours a week, gym classes were unnecessary. At Pembroke School, physical education classes averaged approximately thirty students, so excusing athletes would reduce class size significantly, which both Bob and Molly saw as a benefit. The principal, Ben Lewis, was less enthusiastic as these students would only increase the numbers in the study halls. Still, Dennis knew that if Bob insisted, the principal would probably agree. For himself, such a step would be contrary to his conception of physical education. If gym class was just a time for students to exercise, why had he spent five years of his life in preparation to be a physical educator? Dennis believed that high school athletes needed well-rounded instruction in physical education as much as and possibly more than other students. He personally remembered numerous high school athletes who, after graduation, became overweight health risks. Once they stopped competing, the student athletes no longer exercised, except to leave their easy chairs to walk to the refrigerator. These students needed to learn about lifetime sports, nutrition, and more about how their bodies functioned. To excuse them from class would be to rob them of an essential aspect of their education, and Dennis was ready to "go to war" over the ruling.

This was only one of the questions that would create controversy when he presented his proposed curriculum to his colleagues and the administration. Prior to writing the final document, he made the following list of changes he would be proposing:

1 Emphasis on lifetime sports rather than team sports.
2. The need to include new budget categories (e.g., equipment for cross country skiing, tennis, funds for golf greens fees, and the cost of bowling).

3. A planned grade-level curriculum that outlined activities built upon what was learned in previous years.
4. Required instruction in anatomy, physiology, and nutrition.
5. Periodic physical assessments.
6. Occasional written tests.
7. A grading system based on personal growth rather than current skills.
8. Special programs for the physically handicapped.

These new ideas, along with his opposition to excusing athletes from physical education classes, would undoubtedly make for some heated discussion. While Dennis knew that this was the year he was to be reviewed for tenure, he also felt strongly that this requested reevaluation of the curriculum was an important opportunity to bring about change. He saw it as his professional duty to ensure that physical education became a legitimate and important element of the curriculum of his school.

POSSIBLE DISCUSSION QUESTIONS

1. What do you feel should be the appropriate areas of emphasis in physical education classes?

2. Should interscholastic athletes be excused from gym classes?

3. How do you think Dennis should go about bringing change to his department?

Case Study 31

I Didn't Know What to Say!

No issue has been more controversial in our public schools than the subject of religion, and all educators must keep abreast of the changing laws concerning the relationship between church and state. Whether it is the question of prayer in school, Christmas music, or school-sponsored baccalaureates, the issue can be very emotional. Many Christians are convinced that our schools have gone beyond neutrality and have become antagonistic to their religion.

Of all the religious issues, perhaps the most highly contested dispute has been the origin and development of life on earth. Beginning with the famous Scopes trial in 1927, the conflict between the theory of evolution and the Biblical account known as creationism has been a source of continued debate, and those responsible for the development of science curriculums are faced with insistent voices from both sides of the issue. Is evolution merely one of a number of theories explaining the development of human beings? Should the theory known as creationism be given equal time in science class? What about explanations on the origin and development of life by religions other than Christianity? Teachers have frequently been caught in a dilemma as to what should be discussed in science classes.

Brenda Westgate considered herself a Christian. She had attended Sunday School throughout her time in public schools, and unlike many of her fellow students, she continued to attend church while in college. She also had participated in her church youth group both in high school and in college, and although she did not consider herself a born-again Christian, her religion and prayer life had always been important to her. Like many other modern Christians, she did not always feel comfortable talking with others about her faith. A reserved individual, she would never flaunt her religious beliefs or consider pushing her Christian faith on others. When she thought about it, Brenda realized that during her college years, she had gone through a prolonged period of doubt about the validity of the Christian doctrine. As a science major, she had difficulty reconciling what she learned in her classes about the origin of the earth and evolution with the creation story

104

contained in the book of Genesis. During her senior year, she had had several long conversations with the pastor of the church that she attended. These discussions helped her to reach the conclusion that the two explanations of creation and the development of life were not necessarily contradictory, and he gave her several books and articles written by Christian scientists dealing with the subject.

By the time she had accepted her first teaching position as a middle school science teacher in Trumansville, Brenda again was feeling comfortable with her faith. She had concluded that even though she might always have some questions about her Christian beliefs, in her heart, she felt they were true. She had personally reached the conclusion that the world would be a better place if people could accept and live by the teachings of Jesus.

As a result, Brenda continued to be active in the religious activities of her church and also was greatly enjoying her job as a science teacher. For the first two-and-a-half years, there were no incidents that involved religious conflict. Yesterday, however, she had been confronted in class with a question that was troubling her. The textbook she was using contained a chapter entitled "An Introduction to Evolution," which included a description of Charles Darwin's book, *The Origin of Species,* along with sections on more current research on the theory of evolution. For the past two years, she had taught this section of the course without being overly concerned about any problems it might cause her Christian students.

This year the unit discussion had not been so tranquil. While she was explaining that scientists believe that it had taken millions and millions of years for man to evolve, one of her students, Joan Mannett, had remarked to the class, "This doesn't sound like what we're taught in Sunday school." An extremely intelligent young student, Joan was carrying the highest average in the class. Her parents were both successful attorneys and Joan herself was not averse to being argumentative. When the student raised the question, Keith Turley, another outspoken thirteen-year-old, had responded by saying, "Of course not, that Adam and Eve business is all just a myth." Before she could intervene, an argument had broken out in class and Brenda had had to raise her voice to quell the disturbance. She knew that this was what her education instructors would have called a "teachable moment." Unfortunately, she was at a loss for words and at least at that point, chose to avoid the entire discussion. After the period was over, Joan had told her that she had not meant to disrupt the class, but that she hoped that Brenda would at some point talk about the conflict between evolution and creationism. Responding that she wasn't sure science class was the appropriate place for such a discussion, Brenda promised Joan that she would consider the request.

The fact was that she had thought of little else since yesterday's class. She had reread in her history book the account of the Scopes trial, looked again at the book of Genesis, and reviewed her books on school law. She was still unclear about what she could or could not say in her class. Brenda remembered a speaker in college who had said that if you were asked a question about religion, a teacher could respond. As part of the same speech, the question was raised whether or not creationism could be taught in schools. The answer had been, "Yes, if it is part of the curriculum." Brenda was very aware that there was nothing either in the state curriculum guide or the textbook about any alternative explanation to the evolutionary theory.

Even though it was 8:30 in the evening, Brenda decided to call her science department chairperson, Evelyn Prouty. Evelyn was an experienced teacher who had acted as Brenda's mentor since she began working in the district. Not knowing anything about her friend's religious convictions, she knew Evelyn would not hesitate to share her reactions to the dilemma. The response was unequivocal, "I would not touch this issue with a ten foot-pole. If you have the wrong child in your class and you even bring up religious beliefs, you will be called on the carpet before you know it." Evelyn also mentioned a teacher who had begun an honor society induction ceremony with a prayer that had resulted in a local college professor threatening to take the school to court.

This discussion did not ease Brenda's feelings about the issue and she decided to get another viewpoint. The first person to come to mind was her local pastor. When she called the parsonage, she learned that James Davis, the pastor, was out of town for the next three days. His wife suggested that she call the newly appointed youth pastor, Andrew Streeter. Brenda had looked forward to talking to the older pastor and was less sure of the wisdom of Andrew Streeter. He was only two years older than her and seemed to be quite opinionated and emotional. When faced with the question of how she should react to the issue, he did not hesitate. In his view, "students have a right to know that there is a legitimate alternative explanation to the theory of evolution." He went on to say, "Children cannot be allowed to have their Christian faith destroyed because of the decision of some misinformed judges. The Bible was an essential tool in the education of children when the First Amendment was written." He believed that the founding fathers had no intention of excluding Christianity from the schools, and even quoted verbatim the part of the First Amendment that says, "Congress shall make no law respecting an establishment of religion, or prohibit the free exercise thereof." Getting increasingly more excited, Andrew had continued his history lesson by denouncing decisions that he felt discriminated against Christianity in the public schools. He had advised Brenda, saying, "You not only have the right to talk about the Bible in your class, as a Christian you have the duty to share your beliefs with your students. If someone takes you to court, the church will defend you." After almost a half-hour conversation, Brenda excused herself so that she could complete grading a considerable pile of homework papers.

The two telephone conversations really had not brought her any closer to a decision. Initially, she had simply promised Joan that she would consider the issue, but now thought she needed to say something to the entire class.

POSSIBLE DISCUSSION QUESTIONS

1. Do you believe that religious explanations of the origin of the earth and evolution should be discussed in public school classrooms?

2. What should Brenda say to Joan and the rest of the class?

Case Study 32

The Reference Form

Teachers are frequently asked to write recommendations for both students and student teachers. These reference forms can be crucial for seniors seeking college admission or student teachers applying for their first job. At a time when almost all written recommendations are positive, any suggestion that a candidate for college or employment is less than perfect can be detrimental to the applicant. In some cases, teachers are less than candid with such forms because they fear any comment that is less than laudatory could hurt a student's chances. On the other hand, a teacher who intentionally misrepresents someone's teaching ability could be subjecting future students to an incompetent teacher, and inflated references can undermine the credibility of the writer. A reference form takes added significance when a student is a candidate for a position in the district where he or she has completed student teaching. The problem can be even more difficult when the person asked to write the reference considers the applicant a good person and perhaps even a friend.

Dick Boyd was the first student teacher that Jenny Prentiss, only in her fourth year of teaching, had ever worked with. Initially, she had been reluctant to accept a student teacher, but her principal had encouraged her, saying that he was "confident that she would do a good job." The college had assured John Casper, the principal, that Dick was a very talented young teacher and this assessment had been, for the most part, accurate.

In Jenny's eighth-grade social studies classes, the student teacher had shown great initiative and creativity. Within three days of his arrival, he had urged Jenny to let him get started, and after just two weeks, he was teaching three classes a day with great energy and enthusiasm. The students were drawn to Dick and stayed after school just to talk. He went beyond what was required of a student teacher and formed a United Nations Club. The group hosted a meeting for representatives from area schools, at which a mock general assembly meeting was held. Five different school districts were represented and the day was spent debating world issues.

In class, he had the ability to engage the students in lively discussions of historical issues. Watching him work, Jenny admired Dick's ability to maintain a high level of student interest in the activities of the class. She could see that he would always be a favorite of students wherever he eventually took a teaching position. Along with his ability in the classroom, his interest in individual students was sincere. Even as a student teacher, he had never hesitated to telephone parents to report either a problem or a student's positive accomplishment. Dick did not shrink from hard work. He spent almost ten hours a day in school, and Jenny knew that he was also working several hours each evening at home to prepare his lessons. There was no question that he had won the affection of his students, and it was equally true that he had made an excellent impression on other faculty members. Always ready to joke and converse in the faculty room, Dick's friendliness had impressed many staff members, including the school secretaries and the custodians. Perhaps most important, he had caught the attention of Mr. Casper, the principal. Since Mr. Casper was instrumental in hiring new teachers, Dick had gone out of his way to win over the man who he hoped would be his future boss. To ensure the support of the principal, he had invited Mr. Casper to observe a specially prepared lesson. Sensing the importance of the class, the students had been especially receptive and involved during the principal's visit. Not only was their behavior perfect, but they were attentive and the student participation could not have been better. Jenny and Dick had jointly prepared for the visit and the result had been a near perfect class. There was no doubt in Jenny's mind that Mr. Casper had left the class believing that Dick would make an excellent addition to the faculty. Based on casual conversation and this one lesson, Jenny could understand the principal's enthusiasm.

Unfortunately, there were several problems with Dick's teaching. During his first week at the school, Jenny began to notice numerous spelling and grammatical errors in his lesson plans. At times, he would write incomplete sentences and the problem began to show up in other ways. Frequently, he would misspell words that he wrote on the blackboard, occasionally a student would even correct him. Each time, he would joke about the mistake and suggest that "he was just testing the students." Several notes that he had written home to parents were returned with a notation about his spelling, with one parent who asked, "What kind of student teachers do we have at that school?" After he had helped Jenny with the five-week progress reports, she had had Dick redo many of them because of errors.

As soon as the problem became obvious, Jenny moved quickly to try to avoid future embarrassment for her student teacher and herself. She asked him not to send out any written forms without letting her see them in advance. Whenever he graded essay questions or papers and wrote comments, she found it necessary to check them before they were given back to the student. At times, it was necessary to erase comments he had made on student papers and rewrite them, and he would often totally miss student writing and spelling errors when he graded papers.

While he was teaching, Jenny strongly suggested that he not spontaneously write on the blackboard and encouraged him to use preprepared overheads instead. This technique was only partially successful in that he would frequently write a word on the board without thinking and, too often, the word was misspelled. As early as the second week, Jenny had raised the issue with Dick's supervisor from the college. Dr. Todd had sympathized with her dilemma and he, also, emphasized to Dick the importance of being mindful of his English skills. It was at one of these sessions that Dick admitted that he probably had a learning disability and that as a student, he had never been willing to submit to any special testing. He had said to his master teacher and supervisor, "I guess I just got along on my personality. My grades were never that great, but I always did the homework and the teachers passed me."

Although the college supervisor did what he could to help, it fell on Jenny to deal with the problem on a daily basis. At times, it was very frustrating because she was never sure how Dick felt about the issue. When she limited his freedom to write to parents, he did not balk, nor did he dispute her recommendation that he should preprepare overheads. Still, she had the underlying feeling that he was doing these things because he had to, not because he thought they were important. Several times, she had had the vague feeling that he was thinking, "What's the big deal?" She was not sure, but still worried that once he was free of daily supervision, he would not worry very much about the problem. It also concerned her that during his nine-week assignment, there had not been a great deal of improvement.

After she and her students had had a going away party for Dick, he had given her a reference form to fill out for his college placement folder that would be sent to potential employers. Based in large part on these folders, candidates would be selected to interview in various districts. Jenny was sure that if Dick got to the interview phase, he would undoubtedly receive a number of employment offers. There was no question that he would be perceived as an attractive, personable and enthusiastic candidate, but to get to the interview stage, he would need outside references. She didn't know what Dr. Todd would write, but she did know that most college supervisors seldom included anything on these reference forms that was at all negative. The fact was that her own principal would undoubtedly write a glowing reference. If Dick's liabilities were going to show up in his placement file, Jenny would be the only one who was likely to write about them. There was no question that the young man had many outstanding strengths, but in Jenny's mind, Dick's English skills, especially his atrocious spelling, would be a source of future problems.

Perhaps her greatest concern was that there was likely to be a vacancy in her own department. If she ignored his weaknesses in the recommendation, in her conversations with Mr. Casper, and with the other teachers on the interview team, he might well become her department colleague. She was not totally convinced that this would be good for either the department or the school. There were literally hundreds of social studies teachers available and she wondered whether the school should hire someone who could be a potential source of embarrassment. While she could share the problem with the principal and her colleagues, but not mention it in a written reference, this course of action bothered her, as she feared that her failure to include it on the reference form would be unfair to other school districts. It also seemed that it would be unprofessional. If Dick were to have problems with future employers, Jenny worried that her own credibility as a reference would be in question.

After much thought, she had almost decided to tell Dick that if she were to write a reference, it would be necessary to mention his weakness, but she was going to assure him that the rest of the comments would be extremely positive. Although this solution seemed to be right, Jenny could not bring herself to say it to her former student teacher. Perhaps the reference form had been on her desk for several days simply because she like him too much to hurt him in any way. She knew that the time had come when she must do something.

POSSIBLE DISCUSSION QUESTIONS

1. What are the potential dangers in writing negative comments on reference forms?

2. What should Jenny do?

Case Study 33

Why Do I Have to Grade Them?

How to best assess student achievement is an issue that will always be a matter of great concern for teachers. Schools attempt to judge student work for several purposes. Effective assessment should provide instructors a way to track a student's or a group of students' progress in specific areas so that the teacher can appropriately modify the instructional program. A teacher should use assessment tools as a way to improve student learning, as well as report to parents on their child's academic work, and schools are always developing new grading and reporting procedures. For most teachers, the written test has always been the primary tool for determining a student's mastery of the curriculum, but in recent years, the concept of authentic assessment has broadened the way teachers and schools track and evaluate their students. Some types of classes provide unique problems in the area of evaluation, and perhaps more than teachers of any other subject, art teachers have a unique and difficult task.

The high school art department consisted of four individuals who often had difficulty reaching a consensus on most topics. Ed Spencer knew that the department's assignment to consider changes in the grading system of the school would bring out many of the differences among the members of the department. Currently, Central High School students were graded using a percentage system, but within the school, there were many teachers who wished to return to the letter grade system that had been used in the past. Teachers in the humanities who relied largely on subjective evaluation of essay tests and term papers believed that it was too difficult to justify why one student received a grade of eighty-three percent and another, eighty-two percent—evaluation procedures were not that exact. However, those math and science faculty members who used more objective tests continued to support the percentage system.

As chair of the art department, Ed knew that at least one member, Linda Sands, favored neither of the two systems. She had asked in a recent meeting, "Why do we have to grade them? Who are we to play God with the students' artwork? Besides, if the four of us looked at a student project, we would almost never agree on a grade. This is especially true with our current, ridiculous system." At this point in the discussion, Jon Randall had interrupted, saying, "Are you saying that no one should attempt to judge art? Is one piece of art just as good as any other? If no one evaluates a student's work, how is that person supposed to improve?"

Linda had interrupted with her own question, "Are you saying that students would not do their best unless we held the grade over their heads?" Belinda Smart, the fourth member of the department, had then expressed her opinion that she liked to have the weapon of a grade to ensure that students completed their assignments. She had noted that "I have three classes of basic art with students who are taking the course merely because the state says they have to take a class in art or music to graduate. They don't want to take either of the classes, but they have concluded that it is less painful to take art than to be forced to listen to Beethoven in general music. I need grades if I am going to get them to do the work."

Jon Randall, who was not averse to either the number or the letter grading system, mentioned that in his art history class he gave tests and papers just like teachers in other departments. Again, Linda had jumped into the argument and raised the question about his drawing and painting classes. "Tell me the truth, Jon," she said, "I know that you don't like much about art that has been produced after 1900. If Picasso was in your drawing and painting class, what kind of grade would he be carrying?" Ed could see that Jon was upset with the question, but before the argument got even more personal, he interrupted with this suggestion: "Perhaps we could ask the principal whether our department could use a different grading system than the rest of the school. If we explained that we feel art is different than math or science, maybe Mr. Johnson would be open to allowing us some flexibility." Linda then had asked, "What do you have in mind, Ed?"

Even though he wasn't sure he was ready to share his idea, it seemed that Ed had little choice. "What if, in art, we merely graded satisfactory and unsatisfactory?" he asked. Belinda doubted that the district would allow just one department to have a different system. Ed had been ready for this question and responded that "it might be possible to persuade the music and physical education departments also to accept the idea." Always the practical one in the group, Jon had chimed in with what he thought was the fatal flaw in Ed's plan. "How are we going to average in the satisfactory and unsatisfactory designations in the students' grade point averages? The GPA and class rank are important factors in determining whether a student gets into college. I hope that you are not suggesting that art, music, and physical education should not be counted in the GPA." Belinda quickly saw this as a major danger and she said, "If our art grades do not count as part of a student's GPA, why should we have grades at all?" Without pause, Linda countered by suggesting, "That is the same question I would ask, 'why have grades at all?' Still, I must admit that the satisfactory and unsatisfactory grades would be better than the other options we seem to have available."

Jon had obviously been having difficulty remaining calm and had blurted out that Linda was being "unrealistic." Of course, Linda had bristled at the label and her reaction to the charge led her to mention the fact that her daughter was taking art lessons at the museum and that no grades were necessary to motivate her. She went on to ask about Jon's son, who played first chair trumpet in the band. "He takes private lessons and does he get a grade? I'm sure that he is learning to play very well despite the fact that there is no grade." Jon did not accept these examples as valid and had noted that "these two kids are highly motivated and are very different from the students in Belinda's basic art classes."

Seeing that little progress was being made, Ed decided to float another idea he had been considering. He had introduced the idea by saying, "I know that almost all of us keep portfolios of students' work. Linda suggests that judging art is so subjective that it is unfair to students. What if every student taking an art course had their portfolios judged by all of us and we averaged our marks together to determine a student's grade? Wouldn't that be a fairer way to assess their work?"

Jon pointed out that it would mean that each of them would have to go through over four hundred portfolios. He asked, "Is it reasonable that we should be asked to take on this kind of workload?" Before this idea could be explained, Belinda had chosen that moment to share her own idea. She suggested that "we should not be judging the quality of a student's work, but rather how much that student has improved and the amount of effort put forward. What we are looking for is growth." Before she could finish her statement, several of her colleagues were expressing their objections of grading based only upon improvement.

It was clear to Ed that the department was a long way from reaching a consensus on the issue of an appropriate evaluation for student artwork. He said that he would try to include the options raised at the meeting in the minutes and that the group would continue their discussion at the next department meeting.

POSSIBLE DISCUSSION QUESTIONS

1. Is assigning grades to artwork too subjective to be valid?

2. What do you feel is the best grading system for art classes?

3. As the leader of the department, how should Ed go about developing a consensus among the group?

4. What sort of recommendation do you expect might be agreed upon by this art department?

Case Study 34

It's a Very Good Offer

In the United States, many teachers who work in rural or urban schools are not compensated as generously as those who teach in wealthier suburban schools. We finance our public schools primarily through property taxes, so high wealth districts often are able to spend significantly more money per student for education. In the words of Jonathan Kozol, this creates "savage inequalities," which affect not only the students, but the employees of poor districts, as well. Many who work in these districts do so out of a sense of mission, but that motivation can be severely tested when more lucrative opportunities beckon. This type of dilemma faces not only those who work in public schools, but also those who teach in religious and private schools, and it creates a career dilemma that many excellent teachers face.

Beth Brody had been teaching fourth grade in the Grandview Village School for seven years, taking the position immediately after graduating from a nearby college. Since then, she had completed her master's degree in reading and had emerged as a leader in the school. The first teacher at Grandview to have an inclusion classroom, she had worked to return to her elementary school most of the special education students who were being educated in self-contained classrooms in other buildings. In addition, she had become a consultant for nearby districts after the publication of an article she had written for the state teachers' magazine on how to make inclusion work in any school. The recognition afforded by this article had made her something of a celebrity in her own district, and the local newspaper had printed a story on their first page about her accomplishments as a writer and a consultant. Despite the added recognition, Beth continued to very much enjoy her teaching and up to now had resisted the advice of her principal, Dorothy Hagin, that she enroll in a program in educational administration.

On the personal level, her years at Grandview had been happy ones for Beth. She had met her husband Larry, who was a deputy sheriff in a nearby city, and they had rented a house just a block from the school. Beth and Larry felt very much at home in the community and although they wanted to buy their own home, they had yet to save enough money for a down payment. Each of them had large college loans to pay off and also were paying for the rather expensive wedding and honeymoon they had enjoyed. Even with their rather meager bank account, they were a happy young couple who took a sincere interest in each other's careers.

Like his wife, Larry was very enthusiastic about his work. A college graduate in criminal justice, he hoped someday to be named a detective, and although it was a number of years away, he was not averse to the idea of entering the political arena and running for the office of sheriff. The only problem with his present position was the relatively low rate of pay—after six years, he was still making less than $30,000 a year. Coupled with Beth's $34,500, they were doing fine, but with their college loans and costly trips home to see their parents, they were not doing too well in putting aside money for the future that included having children. Still, they felt that at least in the last several years, they had made a beginning in saving money for a down payment on a house.

Beth's career dilemma began when she received a call from Dr. Don Klausen, the principal of Sandy Creek Elementary School. Just eleven miles from Grandview, Sandy Creek was the most prosperous suburban community in the county and was the home of many professional people. The school district had a statewide reputation for excellence, with about ninety percent of their graduates going on to college, many of them to the most elite colleges in the country. With a strong tax base, the district had been able to build extremely attractive buildings with excellent libraries, elementary classrooms with computers, and class sizes below twenty students. There were teacher aides in every classroom, along with numerous competent volunteers. There were always several hundred applicants for each teaching vacancy in the elementary school. The district seldom selected newly graduated teachers, but rather sought out instructors who had made a reputation somewhere else.

When he called, Dr. Klausen had asked Beth if she would like to visit Sandy Creek, and upon her arrival the principal offered a tour of the building. After returning to his office, he told her that he had carefully read her article and had called her principal to learn more about her. He went on to say that Mrs. Hagin had been extremely complimentary about Beth's work, as well as her leadership potential. He noted that he had talked to Dr. Benson, the head of the teacher education program at her college and he, too, had only good things to say.

In his opinion, Dr. Klausen felt that Beth would fit in well at Sandy Creek Elementary School and said that there would be a position for a fifth-grade team leader in September for which she was perfect. He pointed out that all three of the elementary principals in the district would be retiring during the next ten years, and given Mrs. Hagin's assessment, Beth could "go back to college and earn her administrative certificate." According to Dr. Klausen, Beth would be "just the kind of person that this district would be seeking to lead one of its elementary schools."

He went on to tell her that there was another major reason why he wanted her to join the faculty. Although the school had been into the inclusion movement for several years, it was not going as well as it might. He believed that the ideas she had expressed in her article could make a difference. Before she left his office, Dr. Klausen had told her what her salary would be if she decided to accept the offer. Instead of the $34,500 she was currently receiving in Grandview, her new base salary would be $43,100 and in addition, she would be paid $3,000 for being the grade level team leader. Of course, her current school district had no such position as team leader and there was little or no additional compensation for any professional responsibility. Taking the Sandy Creek position would mean a raise of $11,900, which she figured would represent more than a 34 percent increase in her pay. In addition, the district would pay 90 percent of the family medical insurance plan, whereas in Grandview, the district covered only 75 percent.

All of this had left Beth almost speechless. She had wondered about Dr. Klausen's purpose for inviting her to visit and the thought that she was being offered a position as a grade level team leader shocked her. Somehow, she managed to say something about thinking about the offer and talking to her husband. As she drove home, she thought of all the advantages of this new position. The school was new, tastefully decorated, and had everything a teacher would need. She had observed a classroom briefly and noted that the students were well dressed, quite well behaved, and very responsive in class. During the tour, she had met several faculty members and they, along with the school secretary, had been very friendly, as well as professional. There was no question that the atmosphere at Grandview Elementary School was somewhat dull and uninspiring compared to Sandy Creek.

Although Larry had repeatedly told her how proud he was of the fact that she was being sought out by such a fine school, Beth went to bed that evening thinking that he had never really encouraged her to take the job. He had merely said that he would support whatever decision she made. After hours of conversation, Beth was not at all certain that he was enthusiastic about her leaving Grandview Elementary School.

The next day, she made a point to visit her principal. Mrs. Hagin was aware that Beth had interviewed with Dr. Klausen, and when Beth asked if the principal had any advice, Mrs. Hagin merely said, "It's a very good offer." Although she did not bring it up during the discussion, Beth had heard a rumor that the principal, too, was thinking of taking a position in another district. Of course, this was not unusual at Grandview. The boys' physical education teacher had once called Grandview a farm team for suburbia. Beth had had to ask Larry what a farm team was and when she heard the explanation, she could not disagree with her colleague, as a number of her fellow teachers were now working in suburban districts. Beth thought about talking with some of her friends on the faculty, but could not bring herself to do so. When she called her parents that night, they were both very pleased and suggested that it was a "wonderful opportunity."

Although there were serious doubts in her mind, Beth was drawn by the fact that the position she was being offered would be a great challenge as well as a chance to grow professionally. Still, she knew that before her meeting with Dr. Klausen, she had been extremely happy with her work at Grandview. She felt very close to her friends on the faculty and believed that together they were making a difference in the lives of their students. When she graduated from college, Beth had purposely sought out a position in a small village school and it had proved to be a wonderful seven years. She could not help but wonder, "Why should I give all this up? The children in Grandview need me more than those rich children in Sandy Creek." On the other hand, she thought, "All children need caring and effective teachers." Beth knew that this was going to be an important and difficult decision.

POSSIBLE DISCUSSION QUESTIONS

1. What are the factors a teacher should consider when deciding on the type of school and community one should work in?

2. If you had to make the decision Beth is faced with, what would you do?

Case Study 35

I Just Don't Know What Is Right!

Historically, the private lives of teachers have been a matter of concern for school authorities and parents. Teachers have been expected to be role models for their students and behavior that was considered by the community to be inappropriate could affect a teacher's position in the school district. In recent years, the courts as well as society in general have taken an increasingly liberal view concerning the private lives of teachers. The primary question now seems to be: Does the teacher's behavior significantly disrupt the educational process or erode the credibility of the teacher with students, colleagues or the community?

Whatever the status of the law, individual teachers must make choices that are right for them, and must consider the social mores and expectations in the communities in which they work and live. What one community may accept might create a major problem in another. A related problem is whether or not it is wise for school employees to live in the district in which they work. Teachers seeking additional privacy and flexibility in their private lives might well choose to live outside of their school district. In any case, students, administrators, and community members will continue to take an interest in any faculty member who is engaged in activities or a lifestyle which might be considered improper.

There were only six single teachers in the Lewistown School District who were under thirty years of age. The semi-rural community was a substantial commute from a nearby city, so all of these young teachers were living in Lewistown, and in fact, the vast majority of the ninety-four faculty members lived in or near town. Many were married with children attending the district schools, but at least one-third of the teachers were close to retirement. Although there were several faculty parties each year, the young teachers pursued their own social lives.

Four of the young group who had been living in town for at least three years had become close friends who spent much of their free time together. The social leader of this small group was Tom Edwards, a popular high school social studies teacher. Amy Benson and Jeanette Wayne taught at the elementary school, while the fourth member of the group, Ben Little, was a physical education teacher at the middle school. Tom and Ben had received tenure the previous year and the two women were being considered for tenure this year. The fifth single teacher was Amanda Smith, a high school music teacher who lived at home with her parents. She was a serious and rather quiet young lady who had never become part of the socially active foursome. Amanda was working on a master's degree in fine arts at a university in the city and spent most of her free time practicing and studying. She had gone out socially with her fellow teachers on several occasions, but neither she nor the group had felt particularly comfortable together.

Marilyn Lacey was a first-year teacher who taught English in the middle school. A graduate of a Methodist college, she had had an active social life and had been very anxious to make friends when she came to Lewistown. Within two weeks, she had met all of the other single teachers and was excited when Amy Benson had asked her to come to a card game that night and enjoy the company of her fellow teachers. Having come from a family of people who did not drink alcoholic beverages, she had been a bit uncomfortable when she was the only one drinking a soda while the others were drinking beer. She had experienced similar situations in college, but had learned to accept the fact that many people could enjoy social drinking without it affecting their behavior. With the exception of Ben who had three drinks, the others only had one or two during the course of the evening. Near the end of their game, she had noted that Ben was getting more boisterous, but certainly was under control. When he had lit a cigarette, Marilyn had been tempted to ask him how a physical education teacher and coach could possibly be a smoker. Although it would not have been difficult for her to launch into a lecture about a teacher's obligation to model healthy behavior, Ben was a new acquaintance and she restrained herself from being critical. When she arrived back at her own apartment, Marilyn had concluded that for the most part, it had been a nice evening. That Sunday when she called her parents, she shared the fact that there were some "neat young people on the faculty." Her parents appeared pleased to hear that their daughter was developing a social life. They had been worried that it could be a lonely experience for an outgoing twenty-two-year-old to live in a town many miles from home. Although she did not tell her parents, Marilyn had especially enjoyed being with Tom Edwards. She had noticed that the four friends did not really seem to be divided into couples and suspected that the girls might have their own boyfriends back home. In any case, Marilyn was looking forward to the opportunity for more contact with the group.

Her chance came when Jeanette stopped by her classroom and asked if she would like to go bowling with the group on Friday evening. After admitting that she was a terrible bowler, Marilyn quickly accepted the invitation. The group met at the local bowling alley, which was a beehive of activity when they arrived, and all twelve alleys were being used. Ben learned that it would be a half hour before an alley would be available and he beckoned the group over to the bar that was adjacent to the alleys. He announced in a voice that could be heard throughout the room that he had received his check that day for coaching soccer and that he would buy drinks for the group. All of the tables in the room were filled and Ben invited the three girls to come over to the bar to take advantage of three empty barstools that were available. Reluctantly, Marilyn sat on the stool and began to sip her soda. Over at one of the tables having a family meal she saw the Clark family. Their daughter, Sara, was a student in one of Marilyn's English classes, and Marilyn had recently met Mr. and Mrs. Clark at the annual open house. She had also seen them on Sunday mornings at the Methodist church. Feeling very uncomfortable atop the barstool, Marilyn didn't know whether she should acknowledge the family or ignore them. Meanwhile, she had a feeling that her group of teacher friends were becoming noisier.

At 7:30, the alleys were still not ready, so Tom bought a second round of drinks. While they continued to wait, three boys on Ben's high school soccer team saw the group in the bar and came across the room to say hello to their coach. One of the boys pointed to the beer in Ben's hand and said, "How come we have all these training rules and can't drink, and you can?" Although all of the teachers in the group were uncomfortable, Ben without pausing said to the boy, "You do what I say, not what I do." His remark was greeted with silence and the boys quickly excused themselves and went back into the bowling alley. At this point, Tom had said to Ben, "Couldn't you think of anything better to say to those kids than that?" Obviously upset at being second guessed by his friend, Ben had answered in a voice loud enough to be heard by a number of people in the room, "What do I care? I'm on tenure."

Soon after, the group was informed that there was a vacant alley. Feeling very uncomfortable, Marilyn thought about excusing herself and leaving, but decided that she should stay on. Actually, when the bowling began, she quickly forgot about her experience in the barroom. Her companions seemed to enjoy laughing at her initial efforts at bowling, but she got better with each game and by the third game she was actually ahead of the physical education teacher.

Despite the fact that they were having a lot of laughs, Marilyn noticed that a number of people in the room seemed to be watching her group. She couldn't help but wonder what these observers were thinking about the young schoolteachers. When Amy suggested a fourth game, everyone agreed, and Ben escaped to the bar and returned with another tray of drinks. Marilyn certainly did not want another soda and she was also aware that she had not paid for any of the drinks. Thinking that the least she might do was to get something for the group to eat, she went into the bar and bought four bags of potato chips. A father of one of her students was standing at the bar and asked her, "What are you doing here, young lady? Can I buy you a drink?" Totally embarrassed, Marilyn mumbled something about bowling with her friends and almost ran out of the room. Once again, she questioned the whole evening and whether she should even be in the bowling alley.

After a fourth game when everyone seemed to be tired, she excused herself and thanked the group for the invitation. As she was driving home, Marilyn was aware that she smelled like smoke from the entire pack of cigarettes Ben had gone through. Despite the fact that she had enjoyed much of the evening, she could not forget the incidents with the parents and students. Marilyn remembered well the words of her education professor who had said, "As a teacher, it is not so much what we say that will affect our students, but rather the kind of people we are that will make the difference. Whether we like it or not, teachers will be role models for our students." She was feeling quite sure that she and her fellow teachers had not been great role models in the bowling alley.

This feeling was reinforced when her principal, Craig Johnson, had said to her while they were passing in the hallway on Monday morning, "I hear that you guys had a pretty wild party at the bowling alley Friday night." He didn't stop long enough for Marilyn to try to explain. Even if he had, she was not sure what she would have said. All that she could think was that she had already established a reputation in the district as some kind of "party girl."

The more she thought about her situation, the more depressed Marilyn became. She knew that she wanted and needed friends to be happy, and with the exception of a group of young married couples, she had little choice in making friends with colleagues at school. The four teachers she had spent time with seemed not to worry about pursuing their social lives among the students and parents of the district. She suspected that as a newcomer to the group, she was not going to be able to change their habits, and she had to admit that they were fun people to be with.

If she had been in high school or even college, she would have shared her dilemma with her father. Although he was a nondrinker and a serious Christian, she expected that he could still help her. Although Marilyn wanted to admit to him, "I just don't know what is right," she just couldn't bring herself to call him. She had assured herself that "as an adult and a professional, I can't rely on my parents to tell me how to live my life." When Tom called and asked if she would like to go bowling again this weekend, she had been at a loss for words and had told him that she would get back to him tomorrow. It seemed that she would have to make her decision sooner rather than later.

POSSIBLE DISCUSSION QUESTIONS

1. Do you think that it is wise for teachers to live in the district in which they work?

2. Is it a good idea for married teachers with a family to have their children attend the school in which they work? What kind of pressure, if any, does this place upon the children?

3. What are some of the behaviors or actions that might endanger a teacher's future employment in the district?

4. What should Marilyn do about her problem?

Case Study 36

What Do I Say to the Class?

The death of a classmate, teacher, or loved one can cause a variety of problems for students of any age, and school personnel must be extremely sensitive to the effect of such a loss upon their students. Some schools develop policies to help deal with these events, such as moments of silence for the deceased, flying the flag at half mast, and release times for the funeral. Providing additional counselors can help a school deal with some of the obvious problems that arise, but they do not speak specifically to how teachers will deal with a tragedy in the classroom. Few teachers escape this problem during their careers. The following case studies deal with a death at the elementary level and the high school level.

ELEMENTARY CASE STUDY

It was obvious that Amanda Harris was sick on the first day of school. Her teacher, Connie Williams, had heard that her new student had been undergoing chemotherapy treatments during the summer. Still, Connie was unprepared for the appearance of the girl who only last year had been a healthy and vibrant fourth grader. Having lost considerable weight, Amanda was extremely pale and moved very slowly.

As Connie prepared for the new year, she had read the records of each of her new students. Of all the children in her fifth-grade class, Amanda seemed to have the most exceptional record. Her grades from kindergarten through fourth grade had all been A's and she had already demonstrated special talents in physical education and music. The anecdotal record left by her former teachers described her as a popular class leader and all of her former instructors had found her a joy to have in class. Everyone in the school had been shocked and saddened when Mr. and Mrs. Harris notified the principal that their daughter had been diagnosed with leukemia. Although she had missed some school in May and June because of her illness, it had been determined that there was no question that she should be promoted to the fifth grade for the coming year.

124

When Connie found out that she would have Amanda in class, it was clear to her that it would be a difficult year. After hearing about the case and the diagnosis, a physician friend had told her that it was very possible that Amanda would not survive the year. Despite the girl's regular attendance at school in September and October, it became obvious that Amanda's condition was deteriorating. The chemotherapy had caused her to lose her hair and she wore a wig covered by a kerchief. Although at times she actively participated in classroom activities, there were whole days when she appeared to be listless.

Every day, her classmates made efforts to be friendly and to try to make Amanda smile. Watching her, Connie marveled at the girl's courage. Amanda never complained and even sought to console her classmates when they had problems. As her condition worsened, the atmosphere in the classroom was affected. When she was in school, there sometimes seemed to be a more solemn feeling among the students. As much as Connie attempted to cheer up the students, she too was feeling a certain sadness watching the condition of her student change for the worse. She could not help but ask herself how the loving God that she worshipped in church on Sundays could allow this to happen to a child.

During November, Amanda spent every other week in the hospital. Connie visited several times and on each visit, it was obvious that Amanda had appreciated her coming. It was very difficult for Connie and she found herself crying each time she left the hospital. She knew that her husband was worried about how her student's sickness was affecting her and reminded her that she needed to remain strong for her students.

In early December, Amanda was rushed to the hospital for the final time. Just before the beginning of Christmas vacation, Connie received a call at home from her principal who informed her that Amanda had died that evening. On hearing the news, Connie asked through her tears, "What do I say to the class?"

POSSIBLE DISCUSSION QUESTIONS

1. In the case of the fifth grader's death, what should happen in the school and in Connie's classroom the next day?

2. If there is a memorial service during the school day, should students be released to attend? Should the school provide transportation? Should school be canceled?

3. What special arrangements should be made to help students, faculty, and staff cope with this tragedy?

Unfortunately, suicide among American high school students is not uncommon and when it occurs, it can create serious emotional problems in a school community.

Although there will be much sympathy for the family of the student, there might also be many who harbor guilt in that they may consider themselves in part responsible for the death. There are also those who worry about making the deceased student appear to be a martyr for other impressionable young people. All of these conflicting emotions can create a very difficult situation for teachers in the school.

HIGH SCHOOL CASE STUDY

Lee Payton was a member of the senior class at Edison High School. A thin boy weighing no more than 125 pounds, Lee had long, straggly hair, earrings, and a persistent case of teenage acne. He was a very quiet young man who participated little in class and if he did manage to graduate, would undoubtedly be in the bottom quarter of his class.

Perhaps the only reason the boy had not dropped out of school was his interest in music. As the first chair clarinet player in the school band, he was able to sight-read almost any music written for his instrument. Beginning as a sophomore, he had received an A-rating for ambitious solos at the county music festival. Although he loved the clarinet, during the past two years he had learned to play the electric bass, and the summer before his senior year, Lee and three other boys from the school formed a rock band called Magnesium Torque. The group became the most important interest in their lives. Practicing as much as twenty hours a week, they were able to develop an entire evening's repertoire of songs.

Patterning their musical style on the group Aerosmith, they worked very hard on perfecting each number. After being auditioned by a committee of the Student Council, the band had its debut at a school dance after the opening home football game. Lee and his band members received many compliments from their fellow students, as well as the chaperones, for their performance at the dance, and for the first time in his life, Lee had received positive feedback from his peers. In fact, it was after this dance that Carol Kovaleski began to show an interest in him and by the beginning of the second semester, Lee and Carol were seeing each other often. Carol loved to come to the rehearsals of the group and was present on the three occasions during the year that the band performed in public.

The school band director, Les Nelson, was very happy that his lead clarinet player seemed to be prospering. As he had for several years, Lee spent almost every free period in the music room and if Les was free, the boy would often seek to talk with him. It was clear that Lee had problems communicating with his parents. Several times, he had told his teacher that despite the fact that he had told his parents that he did not want to go to college almost every evening, his parents were "on him" about completing his college applications. Lee had confided that he was feeling so much pressure that he had thought about leaving home. In his own mind, the only future he could think of was a career in music.

Looking back, Les thought that he should have been much more cognizant of the boy's growing depression. In retrospect, there seemed to be three or four major factors that in the end had caused Lee to take his own life the evening of the senior prom. In analyzing the boy's feelings, it seemed that a major problem had been his conviction that his parents would never accept the fact that he didn't want to go to college. If he refused to do what they wanted, he fully expected that he would always be "a loser" in the eyes of his father. Les now could not help but feel that knowing this, he should have talked to the Paytons. Instead, he had merely listened to the boy's complaints and given what had turned out to be useless suggestions.

The second important disappointment in the boy's life was the fact that Magnesium Torque was not chosen to play at the senior prom. The job would have paid the group $800 and allowed them to purchase an addition to their sound system, which all of them felt would make them more competitive with the other professional rock bands in the area. The student committee had auditioned two outside groups, along with Lee's band, and had chosen one of the other bands, telling Lee and his friends that they just did not have the right kind of slow music for a prom. All of the band members were devastated, but none more than Lee, who was both disappointed and angry with his classmates.

Two weeks before the prom, Lee, who had never attended a school dance except to play in the band, managed to work up the confidence to ask Carol to be his date for the prom. When she told him that she had already accepted the invitation of another boy, he was beside himself. Noticing that Lee was talking to almost no one, Les attempted to engage him in conversation, but the boy merely walked away. Preoccupied with the pressure of the school band's upcoming spring concert, however, Les did not make any additional efforts to find out what was bothering Lee.

On the morning after the prom, Lee's mother found her son in his room where he had hung himself, a tape from the band's last rehearsal playing. As the teacher closest to the boy, Les was totally shocked and saddened when he received the news. Mrs. Payton asked him whether he would speak at the memorial service being held for the boy the following Tuesday. She told Les that he had been the only teacher Lee had ever talked about and that the family would be much indebted to him if he would speak. Although he disliked public speaking, Les accepted the invitation.

That Saturday afternoon, the principal invited him to a meeting in her office to discuss how they should react to the suicide. She told Les that several board members had already called her to share their concern that Lee should not be made a hero among his peers. They worried that such treatment might cause other unhappy students to consider suicide. She also mentioned several other issues that the group would be considering at the meeting. Les wrote them down so he could think about them prior to the session:

1. Should the school call in additional counselors to be available for students?
2. Should they begin the day with a moment of silence to honor Lee?
3. Should the flag be flown at half mast, as it had for other students, faculty and staff who had died of natural causes or as the result of an accident?

4. Should there be an assembly program?
5. Should school be called off on the day of the memorial service?
6. If it is not called off, should students and faculty be allowed to leave school to attend?
7. Should the school provide transportation for students to the memorial service?

Along with sharing his opinion on these questions, Les needed to consider what to say to his school band at their Monday rehearsal. While trying to think about all these issues, he could not put out of his mind the fact that he might have been able to prevent this terrible tragedy.

POSSIBLE DISCUSSION QUESTIONS

1. How should Les respond to the questions to be discussed at the meeting?

2. Should suicides be dealt with differently than other deaths?

3. What should he say to the band?

4. What, if anything, can Les do about the guilt he is feeling?

Case Study 37

Somebody Is Going to Get Hurt

Although the use of corporal punishment is illegal, or at the least, severely restricted by law, on occasion, teachers still engage in using physical force to deal with students. Sometimes it occurs out of frustration and anger, but other times, teachers or coaches are attempting to create respect or fear among their students. Whatever one's view on corporal punishment, it is necessary for teachers to refrain from endangering the physical well-being of their students. Teachers who are not cautious in this regard are not only jeopardizing their professional careers, but also placing themselves in a position in which they could be violating the law.

Mike Locke had been a science teacher at Northside High School for five years and took an interest in the extracurricular activities of his school. A football fan, he attended most of the team's games and talked to the athletes about their games and the problems of the team. Recently, he had been hearing much more than he really wanted to about the head football coach, John Fuller.

Even though he had coached the team for twenty-three years, Coach Fuller was seldom seen outside the physical education office. Still, within the community, he had developed a considerable reputation. At age forty-nine, he was still physically quite formidable, although he had probably added at least thirty pounds since he had played fullback in college. The record of the teams that he had coached at Northside was impressive, only experiencing two losing seasons in his long career. In recent years, his teams had won seven league titles and on two occasions had gone on to become state champions.

Within the community, John Fuller was known as an extremely tough coach who demanded absolute respect and obedience from his team. If he ordered an athlete to do thirty push-ups, twenty-nine was unacceptable. A player who brought on a needless penalty could expect a tongue-lashing by the coach on the sideline. Team members were expected to be at practice every day on time and could only be excused if there was a true emergency.

The stories in the community about Coach Fuller were numerous. Most of his former players could share tales about their own encounters with him when they had made a mistake. Still, when the team won a game, a word of praise or even a smile from Coach Fuller meant a great deal to the students who played for him. Tales involving incidences where he had dealt physically with a student also surrounded the coach. There had been very few of his athletes through the years who had not feared to some degree arousing the wrath of their coach.

For Mike Locke, it was the coach's tendency to use physical force that was troubling. After an undefeated championship team last year, this season seemed destined to be Northside's worst ever. The graduation of all but a handful of the starting team was forcing the coach to rely on a number of sophomores on the varsity. These boys were several years away from full physical maturity and their opponents seemed to be dominating the line of scrimmage. Even though the sophomores on the offensive line were talented, they were often outweighed by their opponents by fifteen or twenty pounds. As a result, the quarterback was being sacked too frequently and the running attack had just not been effective during the first five games of the season. The team's problem first came to Mike's attention the second week of school when he heard two of the sophomore linemen talking during biology lab. Dan Galvano, an honor student, had told his friend Pete Snyder that after the last practice scrimmage, Coach Fuller had gotten so mad at him that he had pushed him against a locker and had shaken him for what "seemed like forever." Pete had countered by saying that "the word was that Fuller had slapped Jim Robinson when the second string quarterback had questioned why he had been ordered to do two extra laps around the track." The boys had agreed that Coach Fuller just didn't like to lose and vowed that they were going to do whatever they could to stay on his good side.

Mike remembered that first conversation when, two weeks later, a junior offensive tackle, Tom Kerrary, confided to him that he had had a "terrible run-in with the coach" the day before. Tom had had two holding penalties during the game the previous Saturday night and after a furious reprimand from the coach, the boy had been questioned if he understood. Tom had responded, "I would have to be pretty stupid not to understand. You have just said the same thing six times and called me six different names." With that, the coach had exploded and slapped the student while shouting, "Don't get smart with me, you little SOB!" Tom told Mike that even though it had hurt and cut his lip, he had "stood toe-to-toe with the coach for a few seconds." The boy reported that "this time, I walked away, but if it happens again, I will defend myself. A lot of the guys are getting tired of being pushed around by that big, fat bully!"

Alarmed at this story, Mike decided he needed to say something in order to head off a serious incident in the school. He determined to talk to Mitch Bennett, the district's athletic director, a friendly man who might find a way to diplomatically intervene with the coach. Mitch had listened attentively to his accounts of the incidents that had come to Mike's attention. The athletic director appeared to be concerned and had suggested that the coach was having a terrible time adjusting to losing. In addition, he confided to Mike that the coach was having marital problems and this might be affecting his behavior. It had bothered the young teacher that the athletic director had said that "this is not the first time we have had this problem, but we have always been able to resolve it in the past." Still, as a result of the conversation, it was Mike's impression that something would be done.

Thinking that he had done all that could be expected of him, Mike forgot about the issue until the Monday after the team had suffered a thirty-to-seven loss to their arch rival, Southside High School. Again, Tom confided in his teacher by describing the confrontation in the locker room after the game. The coach had verbally berated at least six individual underclassmen on the team, and with several, shook them while he was making his point. While making his rounds, he had stared at Tom, but did not speak to him. The boy told Mike that about ten of the team members were going to meet at the YMCA that evening to decide what they should do about the coach. He did say that "one thing is clear, we will not take any more of his abuse."

After this conversation, Mike was at a loss as to what to do. He could try talking to Coach Fuller himself, since it was obvious that the athletic director had been unsuccessful in affecting the situation. A second alternative would be to go to Mrs. Clancy, the high school principal, who was an effective principal, but had little interest in the football program. Mike expected that sharing all that he had heard with the principal would in the end anger both the coach and the athletic director. Still, he was worried that if he did nothing, the situation could lead to someone getting hurt. He often worked out at the YMCA himself and thought about casually dropping by while the students were meeting. Even if he did join them, he wasn't sure what he should say. Of course, he could just conclude that none of this was any of his business and forget the whole thing.

POSSIBLE DISCUSSION QUESTIONS

1. Do you think that corporal punishment should be legal in schools? Why? Why not?

2. If it is to be legal, under what circumstances should it be administered?

3. Do teachers have any responsibility in helping to police the behavior of colleagues?

4. What should Mike do in this situation?

The New Student

One child can have a great deal of impact on a classroom, especially when a new student joins the group after a positive environment has been achieved. Teachers must find ways to integrate within their class an increasingly diverse cross-section of children. This is exceptionally difficult at a time when academic grouping is becoming less prevalent and students with various abilities and backgrounds are assigned to the same classroom. Along with the integration of special education students, today's classrooms better reflect the entire spectrum of our society. The result is that teachers need to be particularly sensitive to students who might be significantly different from their peers. It has become a formidable challenge to create a true family-like relationship in the classroom.

Melissa Hill had taught in the Woodcliff Elementary School for eight years. It was Melissa's first teaching position, and she and her husband Larry were happy living in the small suburban district of upper middle class families. Looking back, she was aware that her first three years as a teacher had been quite difficult. As a single teacher, she had worked late most evenings, doing lesson plans and grading papers. Weekends had also found her busy creating projects for her fourth-grade students. A perfectionist, she had never been completely satisfied with the way her class was progressing, and there had frequently been students who had created serious problems. With the many interruptions for special classes, Melissa had never been satisfied with her daily schedule. Always experimenting, it had taken her most of her eight years in the district to develop a weekly schedule and a behavior management plan that satisfied her.

This year, her class was the best that she had ever had. Although there was a range of ability levels, there were no serious discipline problems and most of the time, the children got along beautifully together. Melissa couldn't remember raising her voice during the entire year. She had told Larry the class was too good to be true. The schedule was working well because so few of the students were being "pulled out" for specials such as speech, physical therapy, and remedial reading. Socially, the children appeared to be from families who cared about them. At the fall open house, she had had at least one parent for each child and during the course of the week, several of the parents were coming in as volunteers. On the preliminary reading test in early December, it was clear that the students had made significant progress during the first semester. It was as close to a perfect teaching situation as Melissa ever expected to have.

It seemed that this positive environment might now be threatened. With one week to go before the Christmas vacation, the school counselor had informed Melissa that when classes resumed after the break, she would be receiving a new student. The counselor told her that he and the principal had decided to place the student in her class because of all the fourth-grade teachers, Melissa would undoubtedly do the best job with the new boy. When she learned the news, Melissa asked the counselor to share with her as much as possible about the student who would join her class in January.

Kenny Malone and his mother had come to register the previous day. It was obvious to the counselor that the boy's mother was younger than most parents of fourth graders. As a single parent, Mrs. Malone had raised Kenny since birth and they had moved a number of times since the boy began school. It appeared that Mrs. Malone had limited financial resources, as neither she nor her son were dressed in a way that was typical for the community. In fact, they were not dressed warmly enough for the cold December day on which they had come to register. They were not only lacking substantial winter coats, but also gloves and hats. The counselor had pointed out that his clothing alone would set Kenny apart from the other students in the class. The boy's school records clearly demonstrated that Kenny had had numerous problems in his previous schools. As she reviewed the records, the enormity of the challenge facing Melissa became increasingly clear. The following were her notes from the records:

1. Kenny had repeated first grade and would be one year older than the other students in the class.
2. He was several inches taller than the average fourth grader.
3. He had scored 94 on the most recent IQ test.
4. When tested at the end of third grade, he had not yet reached a second grade reading level.
5. A previous teacher had described Kenny as follows:
   a. Most often quiet, but capable of being belligerent when upset.
   b. In third grade, he had not been friends with most of his classmates. There had been one other boy in the class that he talked with often. Neither Kenny nor his friend showed very much interest in academic work.
6. The boy was most successful with projects that required some mechanical ability. On one occasion, he had actually repaired the classroom slide projector.

7. He was extremely interested in using the classroom computer and was capable of utilizing the Internet. Kenny had also been willing to use the computer to write compositions. Otherwise, he had always disliked writing projects.

8. Kenny had a temper and had been suspended twice as a third grader for fighting. One incident had occurred on the bus and the other in the school cafeteria. Both times, the boy had reported that the other student had been "making fun of him."

9. Mrs. Malone had reported to the school that Kenny spent significant amounts of time watching television. In order to support them, she was working sixty hours each week. Kenny would come home from school and watch television until she arrived home at 7:30 p.m. to make supper. A neighbor in the adjoining apartment looked in on occasion to check on him. They had moved from the apartment that had been located in the city to a smaller apartment in Woodcliff to get Kenny away from the city atmosphere. Mrs. Malone would be working in the kitchen at the Woodcliff Country Club and hoped that her son's new school would make a difference for him. She appeared to love her son, but feared that she soon would no longer be able to control his behavior.

10. Kenny had also appeared to have exceptional athletic ability. His best grades were in physical education and his gym teachers had written on the report card that "Kenny is a natural athlete."

11. It had been difficult for his teachers to get to know the boy. He did not seem eager to talk with his teachers, although he seemed to have an easier time with female than male teachers.

12. The final comment in the boy's file was from his third-grade teacher, who wrote, "Kenny until now has not blossomed as a student or as a child. He has some very special talents that can bring him recognition and success. At this point in his life, he has erected a shell around himself and intends to keep everything within. He has an anger building up in him that, if not checked, could result in serious problems for himself and others. Although his mother loves her son, she lacks the time or the ability to help the boy. I grew to love this child, but have not made much difference in his life. I can only pray that his future teachers can find a way to make a difference with Kenny. He is well worth any effort that might be necessary."

The comment was signed by Linda Pringle, Kenny's third-grade teacher. After reading her notes and drying the tears that had come to her eyes, Melissa sat at her desk to think about her challenge. She had one week before Christmas to prepare for her new student.

POSSIBLE DISCUSSION QUESTIONS

1. What steps should school officials follow to bring about the best possible transition for new students coming into their buildings?

2. What should Melissa say to her class about the new student who will be joining them after the holiday?

3. Besides talking with the class, what else can a teacher do to prepare for a new student?

4. Should Melissa do anything different from the regular classroom routine on the day Kenny arrives in class?

About the Author

Bill Hayes has been a high school social studies teacher, department chairman, assistant principal, and high school principal. From 1973 to 1994, he served as superintendent of schools for the Byron-Bergen Central School District, which is located eighteen miles west of Rochester, New York. He was an active member of the New York State Council of School Superintendents and wrote a booklet entitled *The Superintendency Thoughts for New Superintendents*, which is used by the council to prepare new school superintendents in New York state. Mr. Hayes has also written a number of articles for various educational journals. Since his retirement in 1994, he has been the chairman of the Teacher Education Division at Roberts Wesleyan College in Rochester. As a companion to this book, he has written *Real-Life Case Studies for School Administrators*, also published by Scarecrow Press.